Items should be returned on or before the last d[ ]
shown below. Items not already requested by ot[ ]
borrowers may be renewed in person, in writing [ ]
telephone. To renew, please quote the number on the
barcode label. To renew online a PIN is required.
This can be requested at your local library.
Renew online @ **www.dublincitypubliclibraries.ie**
Fines charged for overdue items will include postage
incurred in recovery. Damage to or loss of items will
be charged to the borrower.

Leabharlanna Poiblí Chathair Bhaile Átha Cliath
Dublin City Public Libraries

Brainse Bhaile Thormod   Tel. 6269324/
Baile Átha Cliath
Dublin City Ballyfermot Library

Date Due	Date Due	Date Due
01. OCT 13		
10 MAR 2014		

The Morpeth Roll

Ireland identified in 1841

Christopher Ridgway

EDITOR

FOUR COURTS PRESS

Typeset in 11.5pt on 14pt GaramondPremierPro *by*
Carrigboy Typesetting Services *for*
FOUR COURTS PRESS LTD
7 Malpas Street, Dublin 8, Ireland
www.fourcourtspress.ie
and in North America for
FOUR COURTS PRESS
c/o ISBS, 920 NE 58th Avenue, Suite 300, Portland, OR 97213.

A catalogue record for this title is available
from the British Library.

ISBN 978–1–84682–406–7

Printed in Spain
by Castuera, Pamplona

Contents

Notes on contributors

RICHARD VINCENT COMERFORD is professor emeritus of modern history at NUIM. He recently co-edited (with Christian Noack and Lindsay Janssens) *Holodomor and Gorta Mór: histories, memories and representations of famine in Ukraine and Ireland* (2012).

PATRICK COSGROVE recently finished a postdoctoral research fellowship at NUIM, on the 1841 Irish testimonial to Lord Morpeth. His recent publications include *The Ranch War in Riverstown, Co. Sligo, 1908: 'a reign of terror, intimidation and boycotting'* (2012).

PAUL HOARY is a practising book and manuscript conservator in the Russell Library, NUIM. He trained under the supervision of Matthew Hatton, TCD, and John Gillis of the Delmas Bindery in Marsh's Library, Dublin. In 1999, he studied at the Smithsonian Centre for Materials Research and Education in Washington DC.

CHRISTOPHER RIDGWAY is curator at Castle Howard in North Yorkshire. He is chair of the Yorkshire Country House Partnership, and adjunct professor with the History Department at NUIM. His most recent publications include *The Irish country house: its past, present and future* (2011), co-edited with Terence Dooley; and *Castle Howard and Brideshead: fact, fiction and in-between* (2011).

Abbreviations

CSHIHE   Centre for the Study of Historic Irish Houses and Estates

DIB   *Dictionary of Irish biography*, ed. James McGuire and James Quinn (9 vols, Dublin and Cambridge, 2009), online version: http://dib.cambridge.org.

NUIM   National University of Ireland, Maynooth

ODNB   *Oxford dictionary of national biography*, ed. H.C.G. Matthew and B.H. Harrison (60 vols, Oxford, 2004), with supplements and online revisions, www.oxforddnb.com.

OPW   Office of Public Works

PRONI   Public Record Office of Northern Ireland

QUB   Queen's University Belfast

Preface

Books, exhibitions and lectures all come to fruition after lengthy periods of preparation and development. *The Morpeth Roll: Ireland identified in 1841* is no different. The idea to research and conserve the Morpeth Roll germinated in 2009 when, shortly after its rediscovery in the archives at Castle Howard, it was the subject of a presentation I made at NUI Maynooth. From this event, which tentatively broached numerous questions about this strange and unknown document, a collaborative venture grew between Castle Howard and the Centre for the Study of Historic Irish Houses and Estates, which sits in the History Department at NUIM. It soon became apparent, however, not only that the roll needed a different form of access if it was to be successfully researched, but that its unique form as a roll, of then unknown length, merited special digital treatment. It was with a sense of relief and pleasure that Ancestry.com joined this collaborative venture shortly afterwards.

All along it had been the intention somehow to put the roll on display in Ireland, to allow it to be seen in public for the first time in 170 years. The willingness of the Office of Public Works, which has been a key partner with the CSHIHE since its establishment in 2004, to participate in this idea by offering their venues to host the exhibition contributed greatly to the development of the project; this was also enhanced by the welcome decision of Queen's University, Belfast, and Westport House, Co. Mayo, to host the roll too. Originally it was suggested that the roll be exhibited in 2014, the 150th anniversary of Morpeth's death in 1864, but the fortuitous timing of *The Gathering*, a year-long celebration of Irish culture, tradition and genealogy, made 2013 a more appropriate year for the roll to begin its tour of Ireland. I am grateful that the project can be associated with this important initiative, even though research, conservation and the exhibition itself will continue well beyond the nationwide celebrations of 2013. There is still much to be done before the secrets of its commissioning and construction are fully understood, and, as a resource for genealogists, its 157,439 names offer a rich source for family and local historians.

The collaboration between Castle Howard, NUIM, Ancestry.com, the OPW, QUB and Westport House, and the assistance of Fáilte Ireland, has signalled successful cooperation at organizational level. But in just the same way as the roll's true meaning lies with the individual names of all the signatories, so too it is a number of key individuals who have helped bring this project to fruition.

In Maynooth, my thanks go to Prof. Philip Nolan, president of NUIM, and to his predecessor Prof. Tom Collins, who also agreed to fund a documentary on the roll. Prof. Marian Lyons, Head of the History Department, has shown unstinting encouragement and support, and made many helpful suggestions. I am grateful to Penny Woods and Barbara McCormack, in the Russell Library, and to Cathal McCauley the Librarian at NUIM, for their assistance and cooperation, not least of all for allowing this strange object to lurk among the Pugin bookshelves for months on end. My thanks also to Deirdre Watters in marketing and communications for helping to promote the roll, and to Tom Johnson of Stopwatch Productions who made the documentary. Others who have assisted include Ciaran Reilly and Anthony Hughes, who supplied me with very helpful information on Ireland in the 1840s.

I am especially grateful to my fellow contributors to this volume. Patrick Cosgrove's research into the moment of 1841 has been instrumental in advancing our understanding of the roll and its context. Paul Hoary has performed what can only be described as heroic conservation work on the roll, and has gained a deeper knowledge of its structure than anyone else. He will, I think, cheerfully agree that the roll has exercised a strange fascination, and he is not the first person (nor probably the last) to become happily obsessed with its mysteries. I am also grateful to him for his help and advice in exhibiting the roll, and also to his colleague Louise Walsworth Bell in the conservation studio in the Russell Library for her work on the opening address, transforming it from a scruffy sheet into something far more presentable but without compromising its historical authenticity. Vincent Comerford kindly agreed to write the introduction to this volume, and during this period, aided by a visit to the archives at Castle Howard, he also has become intrigued by Lord Morpeth. His questions and musings have, as always, been sharp and insightful. My thanks to each of them for numerous discussions – lively, full of curiosity and not always able to reach any hard and fast conclusions: just when we seemed on the verge of answering certain questions a new set of enquiries arose.

Thanks also go to the Heritage Council of Ireland for supporting a seminar on the Morpeth Roll in 2010 held at NUIM, at which a series of papers presented research to date. From these provisional findings, a sufficiently robust platform was established to enable us to pursue our investigations further. This assistance was crucial in helping us to develop our thoughts and fashion the next stages. Without their support, the project would not have come to fruition in such a timely manner.

At Ancestry.com, Dan Jones evinced a belief in the roll from the moment he first saw it, and agreed to its digitization; although by Ancestry standards this is a rather small document. Its existence on the Ancestry website means it is available for searching by anyone, anywhere. Peter Goodwin was very helpful in organizing the digitization and for supplying us with hard copies of the images (a welcome if old-fashioned aid to our researches). Miriam Silverman has spoken at events and seminars and has been most supportive, and, in Dublin, Eric Booth has helped greatly to shape the exhibition and our thinking for 2013 and beyond. My thanks go to David Knox and Louisa Sirett from UK Archiving in Edinburgh, who captured the 652 sheets and nearly two hundred extra images in under a week.

In the course of 2012, two very helpful discussions were held, first with Brian Hayes TD, Minister of State at the Department of Finance, and then with Jimmy Deenihan TD, Minister for Arts, Heritage and the Gaeltacht; both ministers were very encouraging and supportive of the project.

At the OPW, Klaus Unger quickly saw the display potential for the roll, and George Moir and Frank Shalvey have been very supportive in allowing it to go to the Main Guard, Clonmel, Kilkenny Castle, Dublin Castle and Derrynane. Special thanks must go to Mary Heffernan for helping work through the curatorial challenges and for her sound advice throughout, and to her colleague Brian Crowley for assessing the venues and helping with the touring exhibition. At QUB, I am grateful to Prof. Peter Gray, head of the School of History and Anthropology, for being so receptive to the idea of exhibiting the roll, as well as for encouraging me to pursue Morpeth at an early stage in my thinking; and to Deirdre Wildy, head of Special Collections & Archives at the McClay Library, for helping organize the display. At Westport House, Biddy Hughes and the Browne family have responded magnificently to a late call for an appropriate venue in the west of Ireland.

In relation to *The Gathering*, a number of encouraging discussions were held with officials at Fáilte Ireland, including John Concannon, Paul Keeley, Rory McCarthy and Jim Miley; but I am especially grateful to Keelin

O'Rourke for the kind offer of assistance. My discussions with Tim O'Connor, chairman of *The Gathering*, have helped situate the Morpeth Roll in a contemporary context, and allowed me to see how its reach extends far beyond the shores of Ireland. His enthusiasm has been infectious, especially his vision for the afterlife of *The Gathering*, and his firm belief that the numerous conversations, begun in 2013, between the home country and the global community will have important echoes for many years afterwards. It is our shared view that the Morpeth Roll can play a part in this process.

My colleagues at Castle Howard have at times been puzzled by this venture across the Irish Sea, far away from Yorkshire. In fact, the distance is not that great: in the 1850s when Carlisle was viceroy in Dublin, he would telegraph Castle Howard with requests for produce from the walled gardens; these would be put on a train and make the overnight crossing from Liverpool, to be on his table in the viceregal lodge the following morning. In 2010, the roll travelled to Maynooth not by train but by car, and my thanks to Bob Sharpe for ferrying this precious cargo. I am grateful to Anna Louise Mason and Hannah Jones for their stimulating curiosity about the project. However, my biggest debt is to the Hon. Simon Howard for all his support. The roll is still a treasured family heirloom (as Morpeth predicted), and his generosity in allowing it to leave Castle Howard after years of lying in obscurity has allowed it to be seen by people across Ireland for the first time; it is only by travelling to Ireland that its full significance has been unlocked. We have also been prompted to contemplate Morpeth's other great testimonial of 1841, the Yorkshire Roll, which has yet to be properly investigated. The knowledge gained from working with the Irish roll will be enormously helpful for when we come to research, and perhaps display, this second grand address at Castle Howard.

Colleagues in Yorkshire include Allen Warren at the University of York, who, while pursuing his own enquiries into Morpeth when he was seventh earl of Carlisle, has offered helpful advice and encouragement; as has David Gent, whose PhD thesis on the earl remains the most complete study of the man and his political life. In Ireland, the expertise and knowledge of the local and family history communities are crucial in uncovering the stories behind the names on the roll, and I am grateful to John Grenham for helping to alert them to its existence and the opportunities it presents. In November 2012, Mario Corrigan, of Kildare County Library, gave a stunning presentation on how to trace these signatories and overcome the absence of any identifying tags. His successful interrogation of the roll convincingly laid to rest anxieties about how traceable these names were.

For permission to quote from the Mulgrave Castle Archives, I am grateful to the Marquis of Normanby, and to Joanna Ellis for facilitating my access to these papers. To Philip Howard of Naworth Castle, I am grateful for permission to reproduce the portrait of Carlisle by Partridge; my thanks also to Sir Humphry Wakefield, Robert Guinness and Conor Mallaghan. I am grateful to Marie McFeely at the National Gallery of Ireland, Jessica Talmage at the Mary Evans Picture Library and the staff at the National Portrait Gallery, London, and the West Yorkshire Archives for helping source images and for permission to use them. I am also grateful to John O'Driscoll of Strokestown Park. In England, Peter Smith has photographed countless documents, paintings and objects associated with Morpeth, none more challenging than the roll itself. Den Stubbs has shown his characteristic touch and flair in helping to design leaflets and exhibition panels. Scott Sherrard has voiced helpful questions and guided my thinking at important stages. I am grateful to Michael Potterton and the team at Four Courts Press for turning typescript and images into a handsome volume with their customary skill and efficiency.

My deepest thanks go to Terence Dooley at NUIM. Not only has he proved a most helpful reader of early drafts, but I am also grateful to him for his unflinching encouragement, interest and enthusiasm (he too was not immune to the intriguing qualities of the roll), as well as for many wide-ranging and convivial discussions about the roll, Morpeth and his times in Ireland. These were all the better for so often being inconclusive: *amicitia doctrina optima est*.

Lastly, my warmest thanks go to Rosie Wade, who has for many months cheerfully accepted the presence not so much of Morpeth himself but of his famous testimonial – that strange 'bobbin contraption', or 'giant toilet roll' as it has sometimes been affectionately called. Often raising questions that had never occurred to me, her support has been greatly appreciated. Moreover, she too has come to realize that, as an object of enquiry, the Morpeth Roll remains almost inexhaustible.

CASTLE HOWARD
February 2013

Introduction

R.V. COMERFORD

IT IS A GREAT PLEASURE TO INTRODUCE the reader to a short collection of specialist essays designed to facilitate access to a fascinating historical source, the Morpeth testimonial roll. Patrick Cosgrove provides a circumstantial account of the context of popular political practice in Ireland and England within which the testimonial emerged in the late summer of 1841. Christopher Ridgway introduces the man who was the subject of this great complimentary gesture and examines in particular his career in Ireland, first as Lord Morpeth and subsequently as 7th earl of Carlisle; as curator of Castle Howard, Christopher furthermore explains the local context in which this treasure, along with so many others, has been preserved for more than 170 years. In addition to being a document, the testimonial comes in the form of a roll dependent on a physical contraption with a spindle and encasing timberwork. Paul Hoary casts the eye of the professional conservationist over paperwork and machinery; his account sheds invaluable light on the creation of the testimonial and its incorporation into a roll, and is vital background information for anyone consulting the roll as it now becomes available on line.

The decade beginning in 1831 constitutes one of the formative epochs in the development of Irish public institutions, and in the implantation of constitutional government in the country's body politic. The Morpeth testimonial roll, recently come again to light, is a document of extraordinary interest that will enable historians to understand and explain the political impact of this reform politics in a substantially new way. And, beyond politics, the roll provides a rare and remarkably large sample of signed personal names, from across Ireland, in 1841, the year of the country's highest ever recorded population.

Leabharlanna Poiblí Chathair Bhaile Átha Cliath
Dublin City Public Libraries

This host of names is a windfall for the ever-growing number of people at home and abroad interested in reconstructing the history of their families. They are not, however, being offered an easy prize: few addresses are given, and determining locations for the numerous clusters of names will be a task to challenge the combined resources of the local history community. There is sure to be an element of contingency in the geographical spread of the signatures, but it is equally likely that the application of new technologies such as GPS will provide potentially significant revelations.

From the viewpoint of social history, the serried ranks of signatures on these large hand-ruled pages provide much food for thought. True, there are many instances of multiple names in the one hand, with or without the 'X' that can signify either illiteracy or inability to attend for the signing. But the great majority of the entries are clearly written autograph signatures of people with distinctive hands that suggest at least occasional practice.

In the 1841 census of Ireland, 'education' was equated with literacy in English. Returns indicated that one and a quarter million males (and about seven hundred thousand females) aged over five could 'read and write'. The most literate ten-year cohort was that of the ten- to twenty-year-olds.[1] The signatories of the testimonial are probably largely confined to those falling within contemporary definitions of the 'active citizen'. This explains the sadly minuscule representation of women, and it probably means (although this will have to be checked as more identifications are made) that even literate males under twenty are significantly under-represented. So, the constituency effectively available to sign the Morpeth testimonial was probably not much more than one million, and that is to include the significant portion of the population that was allied to an opposite political persuasion. That suggests an approximate sign-up rate well in excess of 15 per cent. Even allowing for a proportion of illiterate parish notables signed for by local organizers, this signifies a remarkable level of mobilization: what present-day celebrity in or out of politics could aspire to that level of 'likes' on their social media sites? The roll pays eloquent tribute to the success of literacy acquisition through pay schools, parish schools and private provision in the decades before 1831, subsequently reinforced with the introduction of the national school system.

The very occasional appearance of a name in Gaelic script serves as a reminder that there was a second language and literacy on the island, but also

[1] *Census of Ireland 1841*, pp xxxvi, 438–9.

to highlight its marginalization at this point in history. Its literature and alphabet were the preserve of a handful of experts also fully literate in English. For the millions for whom Irish was their first language, the route to literacy was through the acquisition of English.

The Whig regime in which Morpeth starred and which is endorsed by his testimonial had encroached in various ways on the interests of the landed class, setting up Dublin Castle and its local agents (the constabulary and stipendiary magistrates) as a counterpoint to the entrenched influence of landowners in local affairs, and proclaiming the principle that property has its duties as well as its rights. Although Daniel O'Connell was not a minister, he enjoyed for the first and last time in his career the capacity to influence government appointments, high and low. He grasped the opportunity eagerly. His ally Michael O'Loughlen became attorney general and then first Catholic judge in Ireland for almost a century and a half, and this was only the tip of an iceberg. John Mitchel and other critics of the Liberator would later disparage all of this as 'jobbery'. Historians have queried whether the reforms of the Melbourne government had any popular impact, some asking sceptically if the promotion of a few Catholic lawyers to the bench really mattered to the wider community. The Morpeth Roll gives us a resounding answer. In a modernizing society, nothing matters more than evidence that one's religion or ethnicity is not a barrier to reaching positions of power and honour, even if one is personally unlikely to be able to avail oneself of the opportunity. Whig policy in Ireland from 1835 to 1841 was the actualization of what Catholic emancipation was deemed to have promised. The testimonial address refers to Morpeth's support 'in the dark days of bondage' (before the Catholic Relief Act of 1829) and how he has subsequently endeavoured 'to impart life and spirit to the cold form of civil and religious enfranchisement'. Without immense popular enthusiasm for the policies his government had pursued, this tribute to Morpeth would have been impossible. No amount of elite pressure could have conjured up this level of support.

A majority of Irish landlords strenuously opposed the reforming regime, but it was sustained by a weighty minority, scores of Whig nobles and liberal aristocrats. Their names in a professional copperplate head the roll (Leinster pre-eminent, Lansdowne, Clanricarde, Headford, Sligo, Dunboyne, Cloncurry etc. etc.). Closer analysis should reveal the extent to which the roll reflects the middle class Protestant support that Morpeth so eagerly sought. The Whigs and liberals from both sides of the Irish Sea who combined to join with indigenous popular opinion to reform Ireland in the 1830s were the same combination that legislated in 1833 for the ending of slavery in the British Empire. In addition to universal reforming zeal, their programme for Ireland also reflected enlightened self-interest. They saw reform, in Ireland as elsewhere, as being not only good in itself but as necessary in order to pre-empt revolution. Even as 'the reformers of Ireland' were creating a rare and incontrovertible testament to the strength of their alliance, that alliance was already dissolving. Facing an incoming Tory government, which whatever else it might do would not ask for his advice on patronage, O'Connell at the age of sixty-five had little incentive to wait patiently for the next change of administration. Instead, he changed the political game by embarking on a campaign for repeal of the union. The Whigs would not go along with this because, firstly, they had come to see the union as the guarantee of property and order, and, secondly, an O'Connellite campaign involved the kind of popular mobilization that was anathema to their political ethos. We can think of the roll as a virtual monster meeting, with the duke of Leinster in pride of place. But there was no place for a Whig grandee on a public platform before massing crowds enthused by marching bands and expecting rounds of populist oratory, as in an actual monster meeting. Deference to ascendancy always weighed on O'Connell. Ditching the duke and what he represented was undoubtedly one of the attractions of opting for the repeal campaign.

The political transformation under way is dramatically illustrated by the case of the thirty-two-year-old barrister, Thomas Davis. His unmistakable signature features on the roll. The following year, he was recruited as editor of a new newspaper, the *Nation*, in the pages of which he elaborated an influential programme of Irish reconstruction predicated no longer on liberal reform, but on the latest continentally inspired ideal of essentialist nationality.[2] It was a formula equally alien to the Whigs and to O'Connell. Nevertheless, Davis never forgot that the infrastructure of a modern nation would be provided by the fruits of utilitarian modernization such as the 1830s had produced in significant measure, not least a national school system. In the historical section of one of his most celebrated ballads, 'The West's asleep', Davis contrived to compliment the ancestry of the principal Whig grandee of Connacht with the words: 'And glory guards Clanricarde's grave'.

If the roll is the monument to a political arrangement already dissolving, it comes only four years before the onset of the Great Famine that shook the socio-economic foundations of the country. The poor law system, which,

2 See Helen F. Mulvey, *Thomas Davis: a biographical study* (Washington, DC, 2003).

with its poor rate and workhouses, proved so disastrously inadequate in dealing with the catastrophe, had been legislated for by an act of 1838. Poor law and workhouse would come to be represented as a crass, heartless imposition on the country. For all its eventual unpopularity, at its inception the system was an integral part of the Whig/liberal reform programme, and it was intended and perceived as being of a piece with other measures forcing landlords to accept their social responsibilities (by paying rates for support of the destitute poor) and requiring them to accommodate the wishes of the wider society (by sharing control of the local poor law unions with elected representatives of the tenants).[3] If the poor law had been a source of immense popular aggravation at the time, it is unlikely that the chief secretary who saw it through parliament would have been the subject of such a warm tribute on his departure from office. So, like all the best sources, the Morpeth Roll shows history to be more complex than might have been supposed.

As Patrick Cosgrove demonstrates, the fact that Morpeth received a numerously signed testimonial on his departure from Ireland is readily discoverable from contemporary newspapers. But understanding of the implications of this fact is amplified beyond measure by the availability of the actual document. The case of the Morpeth testimonial roll at Castle Howard illustrates impressively the value to contemporary intellectual and cultural life of the work of those who, there and in less spectacular places, endeavour to maintain and make accessible the significant sites, artefacts and records of earlier ages. The publication of the roll is an occasion for the expression of warm gratitude to Simon Howard, Christopher Ridgway and their staff for enduring dedication to what may sometimes seem like an under-appreciated service. Hopefully the reception of the roll will be a high point for them all, as its publication certainly will be for many students of nineteenth-century Ireland.

CLANE
January 2013

---

3 See Peter Gray, *The making of the Irish poor law, 1815–43* (Manchester, 2009).

'The unbought and spontaneous offering of a generous and oppressed people': the 1841 Irish testimonial to Lord Morpeth

PATRICK COSGROVE

THE IRISH TESTIMONIAL TO LORD MORPETH was organized in 1841 by Augustus Frederick Fitzgerald, third duke of Leinster, and 'the Reformers of Ireland' to mark the end of Lord Morpeth's tenure as chief secretary of Ireland (fig. 1). It was unique both in terms of Irish testimonials, and as a farewell gift to a departing official from London. The testimonial comprises a farewell address signed, according to contemporary sources, by at least 250,000 people.[1] The extant document, however, contains closer to 160,000 names, so it is possible that sections of it have not survived or that contemporaries exaggerated the number of names for political and propaganda purposes. The document is effectively a pre-Famine census substitute, and includes the names of landed gentry, clergy, merchants, traders and others throughout Ireland on the eve of the Great Famine of 1845–51. The document itself is composed of 652 individual sheets, joined tail-to-head by glued paper strips; this sequence created a continuous length of paper, 420m long, which was subsequently rolled onto a mahogany bobbin. While Lord Morpeth has featured in the historiography of the period, and has even been the subject of a biography, there has been little or no mention of the Irish testimonial roll he received in 1841.[2] An investigation into the provenance of

---

1 See *Freeman's Journal*, 15 Sept. 1841; *Morning Chronicle*, 16 Sept. 1841; *Bristol Mercury*, 18 Sept. 1841; *Caledonian Mercury*, 18 Sept. 1841. According to the Census of Ireland, 1841, the population stood at just over eight million.   2 See, for example, Boyd Hilton, 'Whiggery, religion and social reform: the case of Lord Morpeth', *Historical Journal*, 37:4 (1994), 829–59; Diana Olien, *Morpeth: a Victorian public career* (Washington, DC, 1983). For the Whig administration of 1835 to 1841, see, for example, Gearóid Ó Tuathaigh, *Thomas Drummond and the government of Ireland, 1835–1841* (Dublin, 1978); Peter Mandler, *Aristocratic government in the age of reform: Whigs and liberals, 1830–1852* (Oxford, 1990); Gray, *The making of the Irish poor law.*

1 G. Thompson, *Augustus Frederick Fitzgerald, third duke of Leinster*, c.1840, oil on canvas (courtesy of Conor Mallaghan, Carton House).

the roll, its contents and the circumstances of its presentation sheds important light on Irish perceptions of his term in office and the sophistication of political organization in mid-nineteenth-century Ireland. Furthermore, and perhaps more significantly, it provides evidence of the political mobilization of a broad cross-section of Irish society, from various class, religious and cultural backgrounds, united in their appreciation of the type of Whig government that Lord Morpeth represented.

I

Morpeth was identified as a reforming Whig and during his term of office he carried through legislation on Irish tithes, poor-law and municipal government. From 1835, thanks to the Lichfield House compact, the Whigs were formally allied with the Irish political leader Daniel O'Connell, known as the Liberator after leading the campaign for Catholic emancipation in the 1820s (fig. 2).

2 Bernard Mulrenin, *Daniel O'Connell*, 1836, watercolour and bodycolour on ivory
(© National Portrait Gallery, London).

O'Connell led those Irish MPs who sought to repeal the Act of Union and he enjoyed good relations with Morpeth.[3] The three most important figures in the Irish administration between 1835 and 1841 were the viceroy (Lord Mulgrave), the chief secretary (Morpeth) and the under-secretary (Thomas Drummond). During the course of this Whig administration, some of the hopes raised by Catholic emancipation legislation, which had been passed in 1829, were brought to fruition and a steady increase occurred in the number of Catholics and Liberal Protestants appointed to public office. Morpeth lost his seat in the West Riding of Yorkshire in the 1841 election and, due to the defeat of the Whig government, had to relinquish his post as the chief secretary of Ireland. Ironically, his time in Ireland, his sympathies towards Irish Catholics and especially his relationship with the Irish political leader, Daniel O'Connell, may actually have been significant factors in the loss of his seat.

Upon the realization in Ireland that Morpeth's tenure was coming to an end, a public meeting was called at the Royal Exchange, Dublin, on 12 August 1841. Chaired by the third duke of Leinster, the meeting decided that the eminent services rendered by Morpeth to the cause of 'civil and religious liberty' and his well-known attachment to the people of Ireland entitled him to a demonstration of national confidence and regard.[4] It was resolved that an address would be presented to Morpeth and it was Daniel O'Connell who outlined the scale, ambition and necessity of the project:

> I mean to propose that the address ... be universally circulated, and when that multitude of signatures was procured which would attest the united sentiments of the people of Ireland, and their gratitude towards Lord Morpeth, that the document be then handed his lordship, which he would, no doubt, preserve with pride for his remotest posterity (cheers). It will be the unbought and spontaneous offering of a generous and oppressed people – the unpurchasable testimonial of that ardent disposition which shows how much we value those who are honest and sincere friends of Ireland.[5]

Testimonials were a form of public ritual that recognized and rewarded public service and, as Simon Morgan has noted, 'in the nineteenth century, the key cultural form through which public virtues were identified and rewarded was the public testimonial.'[6] The motivation behind the address to

3 See A.H. Graham, 'The Lichfield House Compact, 1835', *Irish Historical Studies*, 12:47 (Mar. 1961), 209–25. 4 *Freeman's Journal*, 13 Aug. 1841. 5 Ibid. 6 Simon Morgan, 'The reward of public service:

Morpeth was not only to demonstrate 'our cordial attachment towards yourself personally' but even more importantly 'our high respect for your political character.'[7] The address, which was circulated throughout the country for signatures, was very much a political document. Those who sought to add their names to it were affirming their support for the type of government that the Whig administration of 1835 to 1841 had represented, an administration that had not only endeavoured to uphold 'civil and religious liberty' but that was also epitomized by the contemporary slogan of 'justice to Ireland'. As the address outlined:

> During your official career in Ireland it has been your happy destiny to assist in those good measures of policy whose object has been to raise Ireland to a first equality with other portions of the empire. And we venture to affirm that your mind will derive a solace in your retirement from the fact, which we now proclaim, that under the government of which you have been a part, the social state of Ireland has continuously improved and that a more unmixed loyalty and allegiance to our gracious and beloved sovereign have been established than existed towards a monarch, at any former period in history, since the commencement of British connexion.[8]

As well as presenting Morpeth with an address, it was also decided that a banquet would be held in his honour. In this, history was repeating itself for in 1828, not long after entering parliament, he had been invited to a similar banquet in Morrisson's Hotel, Dublin, hosted by the friends of Catholic emancipation, a cause he had firmly supported as a young man. His delight when Catholic emancipation was finally granted in 1829 was manifested in one of his poems, 'The thirteenth of April, 1829', which was named for the day that the Catholic Relief Act received royal assent.[9] The 1828 dinner was chaired by the third duke of Leinster and, according to one newspaper report, the attendance 'consisted of upwards of three hundred persons, including certainly the elite of the aristocratic, landed, professional and mercantile rank, worth and intelligence of Ireland'.[10] This combination of Liberal Protestants and Catholics, working together to promote the cause of 'civil and religious liberty', would also feature prominently at the 1841 banquet for Morpeth.[11]

nineteenth-century testimonials in context', *Historical Research*, 80:208 (May 2007), 262.   7 'To the right honorable Lord Viscount Morpeth, the address of the nobility, gentry, clergy, merchants, traders & people of Ireland', Farewell address, Irish testimonial to Lord Morpeth.   8 Ibid.   9 *Poems by George Howard, Earl of Carlisle, selected by his sisters* (London, 1869), pp 43–47.   10 *Morning Chronicle*, 1 Dec. 1828.   11 Ibid.

In the meantime, the farewell address to Morpeth was made available for signature at the offices of a number of Dublin newspapers such as the *Freeman's Journal*, *Evening Post*, *Monitor*, *Pilot* and *Morning Register*; the public could also sign it at the committee rooms in the Commercial Buildings in Dublin.[12] The secretaries of the organizing committee for the banquet dinner sent copies of the address to prominent individuals throughout Ireland and these were returned with many signatures attached. One such individual was Benjamin Morris, deputy lieutenant for Waterford, who promised to return the address 'in a day or two numerously signed'; while Morgan O'Connell (the Liberator's second son), of Merrion Square, Dublin, undertook to 'procure as many signatures as I can'.[13] The *Freeman's Journal* enthusiastically promoted the collection of signatures, commenting that: 'The address to Lord Morpeth lies for signature in almost every part of Ireland. It is necessary to call the attention of the people to the importance of it being numerously signed. The Catholic clergymen are particularly requested to point this out in their respective localities'.[14] The Catholic Church and its clergy were certainly very prominent in obtaining signatures. In Limerick city on Sunday, 5 September 1841, the address was made available for signatures outside the Catholic churches of the city while similar methods were also used in Belfast.[15] This ensured that the maximum number of signatures was obtained as people went to and from Sunday mass. In Castlebar, Co. Mayo, the Tory newspaper, the *Mayo Constitution*, contemptuously commented that 'two ragged urchins were sent about the town for the purpose of obtaining signatures to an address to his lordship [Morpeth]. They said they were sent by the Roman Catholic curate'.[16] Fr Edward McKenna of Newtownbutler, Co. Fermanagh, gave some insight into the support for Morpeth among the Catholic clergy:

It is admitted on all hands that he [Morpeth] was actuated by a sincere desire to promote the welfare and prosperity of our native land. His promptness in checking local oppression has earned for him golden praises. His impartial conduct inspired the people in general, with confidence in the laws, and has, if possible, increased their loyalty and attachment to their beloved monarch.[17]

---

12 *Freeman's Journal*, 21 Aug. 1841.   13 *Dublin Evening Post*, 31 Aug. 1841.   14 *Freeman's Journal*, 4 Sept. 1841.   15 See *Limerick Reporter*, 3 Sept. 1841; *Freeman's Journal*, 17 Sept. 1841.   16 *Mayo Constitution*, 7 Sept. 1841.   17 *Newry Examiner*, 15 Sept. 1841.

DUBLIN : TUESDAY, SEPTEMBER 14, 1841.

LORD MORPETH.

GREAT MEETING AT THE ROYAL EXCHANGE.

Yesterday, at three o'clock, the deputation appointed to present the address to the Right Hon. Lord Viscount Morpeth, assembled, at the Royal Exchange for that purpose ; and, on the doors being thrown open, the spacious building was, in a few seconds, thronged almost to suffocation. Never on any occasion have we witnessed a more respectable assembly, and we may venture to affirm, that no gentleman similarly connected, as Lord Morpeth has been, with the executive of this country, ever received such an affectionate token. of the love and esteem of the Irish heart as that exhibited at his lordship's departure from this country.

On the platform we observed the following noblemen and gentlemen, who, by their presence, testified their regard for his lordship's public worth, and private virtues :—The Duke of Leinster, the Lord Bishop of Derry, Lord Lurgan, Lord Fingal, Count D'Alton ; Sir Wm. Somerville, Bart. ; Sir John Kennedy, Bart. ; Colonel H. White, M.P. ; Right Hon. D. R. Pigot, M.P. ; Samuel White, M.P. ; James Power, M.P. ; Cornelius O'Brien, M.P. ; M. Blake, M.P. ; R. M. O'Ferrall, M.P. ; W. V. Stuart, M.P. ; R. M. Bellew, M.P. ; Sir John Power, Bart. ; Sir Percy Nugent, Bart. ; Colonel Westenra, M.P. ; Richard Moore, Q.C. ; Leland Crosthwaite, D.L. ; Wm. Murphy, Thos. Wyse, Dominick O'Reilly, Thomas O'Reilly, James Moran, J. R. Price, Peter Purcell, F. W. Conway, D. C. Brady, J. W. Fitzpatrick, Norman Macdonald, Esqrs., &c., &c.

Some hundreds of most respectable gentlemen, who were present, could not find room on the platform.

At a quarter after three o'clock his lordship, accompanied by the members of the deputation, entered the building, and was received with the most heard-stirring plaudits, which were again and again renewed, until the very building rang with the echo. When his lordship ascended the platform, the cheering was renewed, and his lordship repeatedly acknowledged the enthusiasm of the assembly.

On the motion of Lord Fingal, the Duke of Leinster was called to the chair.

The noble Duke then said.—My lord, it gives me the greatest pleasure to have the high honour of informing your lordship, that I was called to the chair on the occasion when this address was agreed to (cheers). The address is signed by no less than 257,000 names (loud cheers) It is signed by 54 peers, 29 right honourables, 25 barons, 97 deputy lieutenants, 12 Roman Catholic bishops, and 472 clergymen of all persuasions, together with the most respectable merchants and traders of Ireland (great cheering).

3 In the library at Castle Howard is a specially bound volume containing press cuttings, inlaid on fresh sheets of paper, covering the events of 14 September 1841 (the Castle Howard Collection).

Daniel O'Connell's recently established Loyal National Repeal Association, whose goal was the repeal of the political union between Ireland and Britain, was particularly active in obtaining signatures for the address. Repeal wardens throughout the country organized and gathered signatures. Benjamin Thomas Parkes, for example, returned 364 signatures from Gilford, Co. Down, and John Sheehy returned five hundred from Ballyheige, Co. Kerry, while Thomas Caulfield returned three hundred from Ballinasloe, Co. Galway.[18] Many wardens were Catholic priests such as Fr Patrick Sullivan who collected and forwarded 1,500 signatures from Cobh, Co. Cork, while other examples included Fr T. Kavanagh who gathered three hundred signatures in Newbridge, Co. Kildare, and Fr John Walsh who collected seven hundred in Urlingford, Co. Kilkenny.[19]

On 14 September 1841, a few hours prior to the celebratory banquet for Morpeth, which was fixed for that evening, a meeting took place at the Royal Exchange in Dublin (fig. 3). The purpose of the gathering, which was estimated at one thousand people and chaired by the third duke of Leinster, was to present Morpeth with the signatures that had been thus far collected and organized in the form of a roll.[20] So many people had squeezed themselves onto the platform that at one stage during the proceedings a section of it collapsed, hurling many men of rank to the floor. Leinster announced that the signatories to the address included '54 peers, 29 right honourables, 25 barons, 97 deputy lieutenants, 12 Roman Catholic bishops and 472 clergymen of all persuasions, together with the most respectable merchants and traders of Ireland'.[21] The organization of the testimonial in little over a month says much about the political organization of the time, especially when one considers the transport and communications systems of that period. Upon receiving the testimonial, an emotional Morpeth responded:

> For all that refers more directly to myself in your address, I thank you most feelingly. I have found among you everything that could most excite and rivet attachment. Through the whole course of my life I shall seize with alacrity any opportunity that passing events may supply for evincing it; and I shall retain this honoured document as its best memorial and incentive, and as the richest heirloom I could bequeath to the name I bear.[22]

Later on that evening, the banquet in Morpeth's honour took place at the Theatre Royal, on Hawkin's Street in Dublin. Doors opened at six o'clock with dinner served at seven; tickets for the event had been set at thirty-two shillings.[23] The Theatre Royal was especially decorated for the event and a band, situated in the upper gallery, added to the ambience of the evening.

---

18 *Freeman's Journal*, 8, 9, 11 Sept. 1841.   19 *Cork Examiner*, 10, 13 Sept. 1841; *Freeman's Journal*, 11 Sept. 1841.   20 *Freeman's Journal*, 15 Sept. 1841.   21 *Pilot*, 15 Sept. 1841.   22 Ibid.   23 *Freeman's*

The upper and lower tiers of boxes were reserved for the ladies. Given the numbers at the event, much of the dinner was necessarily served cold but the sumptuous fare on offer was recorded in the *Freeman's Journal*:

> 60 dishes of soup, turtle &c; 60 roasts of venison, beef, veal and mutton; four dozen of the best Belfast hams; four dozen of tongues, garnished; four dozen of perigord pies; six dozen of prime chickens; three dozen of roast turkey; three dozen of crammed capons; 100 lobster and chicken salad; 60 dishes of gallantins; 40 dishes of bestremeled fowl; 100 shapes of jellies and creams; 60 gateaux de Savoy; there were 60 pieces monte; 60 gilded ornaments; forty high carmels and pyramids.[24]

The venison was supplied by Lord Headfort and the marquis of Clanricarde – who had also brought over red deer from Scotland especially for the event.

II

In order to appreciate the composition, design and scale of the testimonial roll, it is worth noting the precedents for testimonials such as the one presented to Morpeth. The influence of the Chartist movement, and its petitions to parliament, may be seen in the presentation and design of its address, for instance. Chartism was a predominantly working-class movement for social and political reform in Britain, which flourished between 1838 and 1848. Some of the most prominent leaders in the movement were Irish men such as Feargus O'Connor, a lawyer from Co. Cork and owner of the *Northern Star* newspaper based in Leeds, and the Co. Longford born barrister James Bronterre O'Brien. In order to pressurize the government to yield to their demands for reform, the Chartists set about collecting signatures for a petition that would be presented to parliament in 1839. This 'National Petition', as it became known, contained over 1,280,000 signatures gathered from 214 cities, towns and villages throughout Britain.[25] Given the relatively close proximity of the two events, it is quite probable that the testimonial to Morpeth was strongly influenced by the organization, design and structure of the Chartist petition of 1839. The London-based Chartist newspaper, the *Charter*, described the petition as follows:

Journal, 10, 14 Sept. 1841.   **24** *Freeman's Journal*, 15 Sept. 1841.   **25** *Hansard* 3, xlviii, 223 (14 June 1839).

> The petition, which is three miles in length ... and weighing nearly 6cwt., after having been bound round with bandages of tin, and placed on a roller of large dimensions, was deposited in a caravan, in the front of which was erected a framework, bearing the words 'National Petition'.[26]

Due to the rather unwieldy nature of the 'National Petition' and its considerable bulk, problems were encountered when the Chartists tried to get it into the parliament buildings and eventually 'it had to be propelled into the House of Commons like a roll of carpet'.[27]

In 1841, another petition to parliament was organized to seek a pardon for a number of Chartist leaders such as Feargus O'Connor and William Lovett, who had been imprisoned. The petition had even more signatures than the 1839 petition and its estimated length when unrolled was 1,335m. The petition was carried into parliament on the shoulders of eighteen stone-masons and, once inside, had to be rolled along the floor of the House of Commons.[28] Further Chartist petitions were presented in 1842 and 1848. As Paul Pickering has noted, 'the Chartists were the first to collate their petitions prior to submission in order to produce one massive document, which added a new dimension to both the public spectacle and the claims of the petitioners to represent national opinion.'[29] Undoubtedly, those responsible for the arrangement and composition of the Morpeth testimonial would have been familiar with the scale, publicity, spectacle and drama of the early Chartist petitions.

In an Irish context, the presentation of an address with signatures attached was not uncommon at this time. Such an address was presented to Fr Theobald Mathew, the Capuchin friar who took up the cause of temperance in the late 1830s. His crusade against the consumption of alcohol proved extremely successful, with vast numbers of people signing the teetotal pledge; the movement attracted the support of the Catholic urban middle class, the rural poor and liberal Protestants. At a meeting in Lurgan, Co. Armagh, on 26 September 1841, less than a fortnight after the presentation of the address to Lord Morpeth, Fr Mathew received an address with thousands of signatures attached from the Belfast Total Abstinence Societies. This invitational

26 *Charter*, 12 May 1839. **27** Thomas Archer, *William Gladstone and his contemporaries: fifty years of social and political progress, vol. i: 1830 to 1845* (Glasgow, 1887), p. 261. **28** *Hansard* 3, lviii, 740–1 (25 May 1841); *Northern Star and Leeds General Advertiser*, 29 May 1841. **29** Paul A. Pickering, '"And your petitioners & c": Chartist petitioning in popular politics, 1838–48', *English Historical Review*, 116:466 (Apr. 2001), 372.

address, entreating Fr Mathew to speak in Belfast at the earliest opportunity, and signed by townsmen of all denominations, was similar in compilation to the Morpeth testimonial but was much smaller in scale. The Belfast *Vindicator* newspaper described how 'the paper which contained the signatures to the ... address was about thirty yards long. When unrolled, it reached from the platform to the extremity of the crowd'.[30] Another similar, if later, Irish example is that of the William Smith O'Brien petition. Smith O'Brien was a nationalist politican who was involved in the Young Ireland rebellion of 1848. His arrest and trial led to various petitions in favour of clemency, to which over eighty thousand signatures were appended, and on 5 June 1849 Smith O'Brien's death sentence was commuted to transportation for life.

III

An appreciation of the configuration of the Morpeth testimonial roll is critical to any understanding of its contents: the roll begins with the text of the farewell address and is followed by the names of the leading members of the landed gentry in Ireland. To this are appended individual sheets of names (of the clergy, merchants, traders and others) joined together to create a continuous length of paper. The first thirty to forty sheets often contain not only names but also addresses, revealing that the signatories hailed from disparate parts of Ireland. Further into the roll, though, the signatories on each sheet appear to all come from a particular area, town or parish. Sometimes the name of the area appears on the top of the sheet, other times on the back of the sheet; and in some cases a sticker detailing the name of an area and the number of signatures has been pasted on. However, a significant proportion of the sheets within the roll do not have an obvious geographical location attached.

As many Catholic priests were prominent in the collection of signatures, it is no surprise to find the signatures of local Catholic parish priests and curates frequently appearing, particularly where signatures were submitted by parish or region. In many cases, the name of the parish priest is given first on the sheet; in such instances, the problem of identifying the geographical origins of the signatures might be surmounted by identifying the parish in which that priest was posted. The first two signatures from Culdaff, Co.

---

30 *Vindicator*, 29 Sept. 1841. For the growth in numbers in Mathew's temperance crusade, see Paul A. Townend, *Father Mathew, temperance and Irish society* (Dublin, 2012), p. 67.

Donegal, for example, are the parish priest, James M. Davitt, and the curate, James O'Doherty. The names of some members of the Catholic hierarchy, including John Murphy, bishop of Cork, also feature. Members of the established church, including Revd James Smith, rector, Island Magee, Belfast, Edward G. Hudson, dean of Armagh, as well as James Cauley, a Presbyterian minister in Co. Antrim, were evidently not averse to showing their support for Morpeth.

From the place-names that appear in the roll, it is evident that there is a fairly wide geographical spread of signatures. However, the methodology used at the time to compile and attach the sheets together appears to have been haphazard. With no organizing principle, the sheets seem to have been conjoined at random, or simply according to the order in which they were received by the organizers; there is no evidence of an overall scheme to group signatories together by province, county, city or even region. There are, for example, several sheets submitted by a J.J. Scanlon, who collected signatures at Church Street Chapel, presumably in Dublin, scattered throughout the roll.

It is important to stress that not all of the names written on the Morpeth testimonial roll are actually the autographs of the individuals named; it is clear from the handwriting on some sections of the document that particular individuals were responsible for writing the names of others. This is also evidenced by letters that appeared in contemporary newspapers; the former MP and mayor of Cork, Francis Bernard Beamish, for instance, sent a letter to the organizing committee thanking them for affixing his name to the address.[31] Therefore, we can be certain that in this instance the signature on the roll is not his own. Equally, illiteracy did not prevent individuals from contributing to the roll, and many simply wrote an 'X' or made their mark beside their name – which was written by someone else.

Research to date would appear to indicate that the signatures on the roll are predominantly male. However, a few women's names have been uncovered: the name 'Mary Ray' appears underneath the signature of T.M. Ray, the secretary of the Loyal National Repeal Association, for example. The women of Ireland may have been quite eager to avail of the opportunity to express their gratitude to Morpeth. Once, while canvassing in Yorkshire, he had landed himself in difficulty by proclaiming that Irish women were more chaste than their English counterparts.[32] While this certainly did not endear

31 *Cork Examiner*, 13 Sep. 1841.   32 *Hansard* 3, xcviii, 220 (11 Apr. 1848).

4 One of Bianconi's excursion cars outside Hearn's Hotel in Clonmel, Co. Tipperary, in 1856. These would have carried sheets of signatures to Dublin in the summer of 1841 (Mary Evans Picture Library).

Morpeth to the women of England, it is enough to raise the hope that some of their counterparts in Ireland managed to sign the testimonial.

Given that the writing of names was not always undertaken by the persons named, there is some duplication of names on the roll. There are, for example, several appearances of the name Daniel O'Connell. One of these occurs on the sheet bearing the signature of T.M. Ray; the other occurs elsewhere in a different hand and followed by the initials 'M.P.' (There is, of course, every possibility that the former is the signature of Daniel O'Connell's son Daniel.) Another interesting signatory is that of Charles Bianconi, an Italian immigrant who came to Ireland in 1802 (figs 4, 5). He revolutionized public transport in Ireland by establishing regular horse-drawn carriage services on various routes from about 1815 onwards. He established a network of routes, which eventually covered most of the country from north to south. Owing to

5 Bianconi's signature on the second sheet of signatories. He also wrote down his home town, Clonmel.

his system of transport, rural Ireland became much more accessible; this, in turn, stimulated trade and helped to reduce the price of many commodities.[33]

While the vast majority of text on the roll is in the English language, a small number of signatures in Gaelic script have been found. Although the

33 'Bianconi' in S.J. Connolly ed., *Oxford companion to Irish history* (2nd ed., Oxford, 2007), p. 48; *DIB*, i, pp 518–20.

6 Sir Frederic William Burton, *Thomas Davis*, graphite on paper
(© National Gallery of Ireland).

Irish language declined significantly after the Great Famine of 1845–51, a significant proportion of the population spoke Irish as their first language in 1841.[34] English, however, was the language of power, commerce and politics, but it is possible that these signatories may have been making a statement by signing their names in Irish. The Young Ireland movement, whose members

34 Brian O'Cuív, 'Irish language and literature' in William Vaughan (ed.), *A new history of Ireland, vi: Ireland under the union, 1870–1921* (Oxford, 1989), pp 385–435.

7 Thomas Davis' signature on the fourth sheet of the roll, recording his name and address at 61 Baggot Street, Dublin.

comprised both Catholics and Protestants from middle-class backgrounds, was a nationalist group that was also in favour of reviving the Irish language. One such member was Thomas Davis, who was born in Mallow, Co. Cork, in 1814 (figs 6, 7). He was the son of a British Army surgeon, who died before he was born, and an Irish Protestant mother. In 1842, he co-founded the *Nation* newspaper and became its editor, publicizing his theories of self-government through articles on Irish history and culture. Davis later became the leader of the Young Ireland movement, but died from scarlet fever in 1845 just three years before the failed Young Ireland rebellion of 1848.[35] Another member of the Young Ireland movement, whose name appears on the roll, was Charles Gavan Duffy. Born in Co. Monaghan of a middle-class Catholic family, he became a journalist and was appointed editor of the Belfast *Vindicator* in 1839 (figs 8, 9). Along with Davis, he was involved with the *Nation* newspaper and in 1844 he was arrested for sedition. He supported the

35 Entry in Connolly (ed.), *Oxford companion*, p. 145; *DIB*, iii, pp 82–6.

8 Charles Gavan Duffy in 1848 (Mary Evans Picture Library).

Young Ireland rebellion of 1848 and was imprisoned as a consequence; upon his release, he emigrated to Australia where he became a very prominent politician.[36]

Aside from names, addresses and, in some cases, occupations, some of the sheets that comprise the roll include comments or remarks with political

36 Entry in Connolly (ed.), *Oxford companion*, p. 173; *DIB*, iii, pp 505–9.

9 Duffy's name appears as 'Charles G. Duffey' with a Belfast location on a sheet transcribed in a uniform hand, but containing individuals from as far afield as Navan, Drogheda, Waterford, Limerick and Roscommon.

connotations. One such comment is that of James P. Ward of Co. Galway, who signed himself a 'Volunteer of 1782'. The Volunteers were a part-time, predominantly Protestant, military force raised during the years 1778 to 1789 in order to defend Ireland against a possible French invasion. Most of the troops regularly stationed in the country had been sent to fight in the American War of Independence. Independent of government control and with an estimated membership of sixty thousand by May 1782, the Volunteers began to gain political influence. After agitation by the Volunteers and by a parliamentary grouping under the leadership of Henry Grattan, greater autonomy and powers were granted to the Irish parliament. These concessions became known as 'the constitution of 1782'. The eighteen years of governance between the granting of 'legislative independence' to the Irish parliament in 1782 and that parliament's abolition by the Act of Union in 1800 have become known as Grattan's Parliament; significantly the name of Grattan's son Henry appears beneath that of 'James P. Ward Volunteer of 1782'.[37]

IV

While Morpeth was undoubtedly personally popular, the testimonial and its voluminous signatures were perhaps less a personal tribute to him and more a tribute to the type of Whig government and policies he represented. It is in this context that the investigation of the provenance of the testimonial, its composition and contents, as well as the circumstances of its presentation, can shed light on Irish perceptions of British governance in the crucial years before the Great Famine. The rapid and widespread collection of names demonstrated the formidable organizational power of O'Connell's network of repeal wardens, the Catholic clergy and the Whig landed gentry. While signing the Morpeth testimonial was clearly a political act on the part of individuals, it is also empirical evidence of mass political involvement in mid-nineteenth-century Ireland. Moreover, the fact that members of the Young Ireland movement signed this testimonial to a British government official, when within a few years they would be involved in an armed rebellion against the crown, is particularly noteworthy, and may be an indicator that the political divisions in Ireland in this period were much more fluid than has been previously thought. The organization and presentation of the testimonial was not just a source of external pressure on an incoming Tory government, but it was also a symbol of the Whig-Irish alliance, reinforcing a sense of collective identity at a time when the Tories were taking up the reins of power, and a gesture of defiance following an election defeat. As the *Manchester Times and Gazette* commented in the aftermath of the presentation of the Irish testimonial roll, 'To speak of a party commanding such an array as this, as insignificant or declining, is sheer folly or effrontery.'[38]

When one considers that many of those who added their names to the address were probably disenfranchised, the addition of their name was perhaps a replacement or alternative method of expressing their political views and support. Indeed, the act of collective participation gave people a stake or shareholding in the testimonial. This unique historical document has enormous research potential, whether looked at as a pre-Famine census

37 *DIB*, iv, pp 205–6.   38 *Manchester Times and Gazette*, 25 Sept. 1841.

substitute, a genealogy resource, a family heirloom, an index of Irish surnames, a directory of who was who in Ireland at the time, or a politically motivated document in its own right. Undoubtedly, future case studies of communities or individuals whose names are documented will reveal more about the 'generous and oppressed people' who made this 'unbought and spontaneous offering' to Lord Morpeth in 1841.

Ireland's favourite Englishman?

CHRISTOPHER RIDGWAY

WHO WAS LORD MORPETH?

I N MAY 1835, George Howard, viscount Morpeth (1802–64), took up the post of chief secretary of Ireland in Lord Melbourne's Whig adminis-tration (fig. 10). Over the next five years, Morpeth, together with viceroy Lord Mulgrave, and under secretary Thomas Drummond would usher in an age of conciliation and rapprochement with Irish MPs, and oversee significant pieces of legislation that went some way towards ameliorating political and social wrongs in the country (figs 11, 12).[1] Their progress was anything but smooth or straightforward. During their tenure, Mulgrave, Morpeth and Drummond would regularly experience the criticism of political colleagues and foes, as well as the opprobrium of sections of the press, as they introduced and reintroduced legislation dealing with tithe and municipal reform, a poor law for Ireland and positive action to redress the imbalances between Protestant and Catholic appointees in official posts. By July 1835, after only weeks in office, Morpeth had encountered sufficient hostility for him to remark in a letter to Mulgrave, 'I begin to get much anonymous vituperation, threatening me with much here and much hereafter'.[2]

Mulgrave left Dublin in 1839 to take up the post of secretary for war and the colonies; in 1840, Drummond, aged forty-two, died from erysipelas, a bacterial skin infection;[3] and a year later, Morpeth left office after losing his parliamentary seat in the general election. The fall of the Whig government in 1841 brought to an end a special period of close working between London and Dublin, shaped not only by liberal attitudes among the Whigs but by a

1 Constantine Henry Phipps (1797–1863) was born the second earl of Mulgrave and created first marquess of Normanby in 1838. He is referred to throughout as Lord Mulgrave. *ODNB*, xliv, pp 176–8. 2 Morpeth to Mulgrave, 2 July 1835, Mulgrave Castle MSS, M/469. 3 *ODNB*, xvi, pp 981–6.

10 Thomas Carrick, *George Howard, Lord Morpeth, c.*1835, watercolour (the Castle Howard Collection).

2

8

 The Morpeth Roll

11 Daniel Maclise, *Constantine Henry Phipps, first marquess of Normanby*, 1835, pen and ink (© National Portrait Gallery, London).

12 Henry Cousins, after Henry William Pickersgill, *Thomas Drummond*, 1841
(the Castle Howard Collection).

strategic alliance with Daniel O'Connell and his Repeal party. Future premier
Lord John Russell was to describe the 1830s as a 'sweet sleep' when 'Irish
agitation slumbered'; and, while agrarian unrest and murder were not
unknown, the decade was a relatively peaceful one.[4]

4 Quoted in Boyd Hilton, *A mad, bad & dangerous people? England, 1783–1846* (Oxford, 2006), p. 538.
Although the Tithe War witnessed outbursts of violence, Gearóid Ó Tuathaigh considers the later 1830s
to have been remarkably calm: *Thomas Drummond*, p. 22.

The Right Honourable
Lord Viscount Morpeth

THE ADDRESS
of the
Nobility, Gentry, Clergy, Merchants, Traders &
PEOPLE of IRELAND

My Lord

We The Reformers of Ireland convened by Public Requisition, for the purpose of considering the most suitable means of manifesting our high respect for your Political Character, and our cordial attachment towards yourself personally, cannot permit Your Lordship (with our recollection of recent events) to terminate that Official Connexion with our Country, which has happily existed for more than six years, without tendering to Your Lordship formally, the assurance of the profound respect and affection which we entertain towards Your Lordship.

We held in our grateful remembrance the devoted zeal with which, in early life — in those dark days of bondage, when a vast majority of our fellow Countrymen were oppressed for Conscience sake — Your Lordship ranged yourself with the Friends of Ireland — And we have marked the earnestness with which Your Lordship has ever since essayed to impart life and spirit to the well form of Civil and Religious Enfranchisement, which you and others had created.

During your Official career in Ireland, it has been your happy destiny to assist in those good measures of Policy, whose object has been to raise Ireland to a foot of equality with other portions of the Empire — And we venture to affirm that your mind will derive a solace on your retirement from the fact which we now proclaim, that under the Government of which you have been a part, the social state of Ireland has continuously improved, and that a more assured Loyalty and Allegiance to Her Gracious and Beloved Sovereign have been established, than existed towards a Monarch, at any former period in history, since the commencement of British Connexion.

To recapitulate the various Acts of Public Service which Your Lordship has accomplished in Ireland, would far exceed the limits prescribed to an occasion like the present — to enumerate the beneficent designs in which Your Lordship has been engaged, but which have been instead abortive by the hostility of the Enemies of Ireland, would still more transcend the boundary which we have defined for our immediate purpose — Let Your Lordship be assured, that the People of Ireland treasure in their Hearts, the recollection of every benefit designed for the amelioration of their Country.

To such of us as have enjoyed the opportunity of personal communication with Your Lordship, it may be permitted to express our fond recollection of the kindliness of disposition, and the frank and courteous Demeanour which adorn your private intercourse — eminent indeed must be those qualities, to which we, your Friends, adjust, when their existence in your person, wrung even from your Adversaries, a full acknowledgment.

We cannot retire from Your Lordships presence without adverting to the recent event, which has removed Your Lordship from the House of Commons and giving expression to our hope, that no temporary impediment may turn Your Lordship from those walks of honor and Public Service, in which it has hitherto been your pride to travel — It may be My Lord that in this hope there lurks some element, not entirely free from Selfishness — there are not times, My Lord, when Ireland can spare from her friendly ranks, A Defender so

13 The opening address to the Morpeth Roll from 'The Reformers of Ireland'
(the Castle Howard Collection).

When Morpeth left Ireland in September 1841 he received an extraordinary and unique farewell gift in the form of a huge testimonial. Reportedly containing more than 250,000 signatures, this testimonial came in the form of an enormous roll, formed of 652 sheets of paper stuck together and wrapped around a gigantic bobbin, and measuring 420m in length. The roll opened with an effusive address full of expressions of gratitude and affection for this departing British official, and closed by assuring Morpeth that 'the warmest good wishes of our country will ever accompany you, in your future progress through life' (fig. 13). Thus, in just six years Morpeth had gone from receiving anonymous 'vituperation' and threats to an outpouring of 'respect', 'affection' and 'grateful remembrance', accompanied by the signatures and names of thousands of individuals. This was an extraordinary turn-around in affairs, and the Morpeth Roll remains unique as a personal testimonial, not only on account of its size but also its form. The sheets of paper are wrapped around the bobbin that sits inside a chest; the two bobbin spindles sit in brass brackets that allow it to turn or spool and so enable the document to unroll as a continuous length. The Morpeth Roll is therefore a grand document *and* a mechanical object (fig. 14).

Why Morpeth should have been so unusually popular in Ireland is something that deserves explanation. This branch of the Howard family was not especially renowned in British, let alone Irish, political affairs. While the third earl of Carlisle (1669–1738) was a figure in the court of William III, becoming privy councillor and first lord of the treasury, his main claim to fame was commissioning the celebrated architect Sir John Vanbrugh to build his exuberant Baroque mansion Castle Howard in 1699; the first private house in England to be crowned with a large and spectacular dome (fig. 15). His son Henry, fourth earl (1694–1758), and grandson Frederick, fifth earl (1748–1825), are best remembered for filling Castle Howard with a profusion of art treasures garnered from Grand Tour travels to Italy (fig. 16). However, the fifth earl did enjoy a political career, appointed by Lord North in 1778 as head of the diplomatic mission to negotiate with the American colonists. Then, in 1780, he arrived in Dublin as viceroy, and while his aloof manner alienated some, he was also sympathetic to the Volunteers but wary of the consequences of legislative independence. Within two years, just before his recall to England, and on the eve of Grattan's Parliament, he was to write presciently:

14 The chest and bobbin transform the long scroll into a mechanical object.

15 Castle Howard, North Yorkshire, home to the Howard family since it was built by Sir John Vanbrugh at the beginning of the eighteenth century.

> It is beyond a doubt that the practicability of governing Ireland by English laws is become utterly visionary; it is with me equally beyond a Doubt that Ireland may be well and happily governed by its own laws.[5]

James Gandon's bridge spanning the Liffey, erected in 1791–5, was for a while named Carlisle Bridge, before it was rebuilt and renamed O'Connell Bridge in the 1870s. The sixth earl (1773–1848), who entered the House of Commons in 1795, had supported the union and aspired to follow in his father's footsteps as viceroy. In 1812, he introduced a motion on the state of Ireland arguing for Catholic relief and urging for 'a sincere and cordial conciliation'; although it was heavily defeated, he continued to voice sympathies for English and Irish Catholics, and in 1814 spoke out on the need to regulate the conduct of the Tory Speaker, Charles Abbot, who had expressed anti-Catholic sentiments in parliament.[6] His son George, born in 1802, became the third successive generation of the family to be involved in

5 Carlisle to Lord Hillsborough, 19 Mar. 1782, *State Papers*, 63/480, fo. 339. See James Kelly, 'Residential and non-residential lords lieutenant: the viceroyalty, 1703–90' in Peter Gray (ed.), *The Irish lord lieutenancy, c.1541–1922* (Dublin, 2012), pp 82–5.   6 www.historyofparliament.org/volume/1790-1820/member/howard-george-1773-1848; *ODNB*, xxviii, pp 351–2.

16 John Hoppner, *Frederick Howard, fifth earl of Carlisle, c.*1800, oil on canvas
(the Castle Howard Collection).

the political affairs of Ireland. Unusually for a grand aristocratic family, these links were not based on landownership; the Howards never owned Irish estates, nor did they marry into Irish families. Their powerbase was always in the north of England, with estates in Yorkshire, Northumberland and Cumberland, with the principal seat at Castle Howard. Thus, their connection with Ireland was through political office, and their status was always one of officials, visitors or temporary residents.

First elected MP in 1826, Lord Morpeth (as he was known until he succeeded as seventh earl of Carlisle in 1848) went on to represent the West Riding of Yorkshire after 1832. In 1835, he joined Melbourne's Whig ministry and was appointed chief secretary for Ireland. Melbourne's administration had achieved a small majority and therefore looked to govern in alliance with Irish MPs. This group was traditionally divided along similar lines to Britain (Whigs and Tories), but the 1830s witnessed the emergence of a genuine third party with the Irish MPs of O'Connell's Repeal party, who had come of political age following Catholic emancipation in 1829. Between them, the Whig and Repeal MPs, together with a handful of English Radicals, held the balance of power. Besides wishing to pursue reforming legislation, the Whigs also needed to conciliate their new political allies. After Catholic emancipation, O'Connell had trumpeted repeal of the union as the next great Irish wrong to be righted, but he was pragmatic enough to know that this stood little chance of coming about. Instead, he was content to secure reform by instalments, always recognizing (and never coy to remind his English allies of the fact) that the threat of mass agitation in the cause of repeal and reform was never far away.[7] In a letter of 7 May 1834 to his political and financial manager, Patrick Vincent Fitzpatrick, he described this tactic as to 'get *what I can* and use the Repeal *in terrorem* merely until it is wise and necessary to recommence the agitation'.[8] O'Connell's relationship with his Whig partners in the second half of the 1830s was a balancing act; it had an improvisatory quality at times with both parties maintaining fixed positions over some issues, while seeking to be flexible and accommodating over others.

Morpeth's popularity can only partly be explained by the reforming legislation passed between 1835 and 1841. The principal bills dealing with Irish tithes, poor law and municipal corporations became protracted exercises in parliamentary attrition. They were debated, amended and passed in the Commons only to be rejected in the Lords, with Morpeth having to

---

7 Roy Foster, *Modern Ireland, 1600–1972* (London, 1988), pp 308–9.   8 Maurice O'Connell (ed.), *The correspondence of Daniel O'Connell* (8 vols, Dublin, 1972–80), v, pp 129–30.

re-present fresh drafts subsequently. When these acts did eventually reach the statute book, it was only after they had been pruned by the Tory-dominated House of Lords. Notwithstanding the meagre and imperfect nature of these achievements, this period was nevertheless seen as a 'brief golden age'.[9] Personality and patronage signalled a change in style of government in Dublin Castle. Mulgrave, Morpeth and Drummond were keen to foster good relations with nationalist MPs. They went out of their way to consult with and, to a degree, listen to O'Connell, and help advance some of his causes and party members. Mulgrave famously likened his viceroyalty to 'the sending of an expedition into a previously hostile territory', and he was pleased to leave behind the harsh earlier phase of Whig government prior to 1835, which had seen the passing of the Coercion Act in 1833.[10] Although not the first viceroy to arrive dressed in green on taking up his post, Mulgrave's flair for theatrical gestures and his bonhomie marked him out as someone different. In a letter to the duke of Leinster in 1846, the duke of Bedford recalled how the period was characterized by 'a good and impartial administration of justice throughout the country' and, unlike former times, rule from Dublin Castle now 'meant nothing but equal justice and the appointment of Catholic magistrates and liberal Protestants by a friendly government'.[11]

Among those appointed to senior positions were the liberal Protestant Louis Perrin as attorney-general, and the Catholic Michael O'Loughlen as solicitor-general. When O'Loughlen was promoted to attorney-general, he was replaced by the Protestant John Richards. This merry-go-round of affirmative action continued when Richards was replaced by the Catholic Stephen Woulfe; and in turn Woulfe's position was filled by the Protestant Maziere Brady; when Brady duly became attorney-general, the Catholic David Richard Pigot acted as his solicitor-general. Other appointments included Thomas Wyse (lord of the treasury), Richard More O'Ferrall (lord of the treasury), and Richard Lalor Sheil (vice-president of the board of trade); while George Evans and James Grattan were made privy councillors. Most of these figures, in spite of periodic disagreements, were associates of O'Connell.[12]

Dispensing patronage was not always easy, and early in office Morpeth likened it to 'an ocean of troubles and bothers', going on to declare, 'the

9 Foster, *Modern Ireland*, p. 310. 10 Mulgrave to Morpeth, 31 May 1837, Castle Howard Archives, J19/1/14/53; see also Peter Gray, 'A "people's viceroyalty"? Popularity, theatre and executive politics, 1835–47' in Gray (ed.), *Irish lord lieutenancy*, pp 158–78. 11 Seventh duke of Bedford to the third duke of Leinster, 28 Mar. 1846 (PRONI D3979/3/33/37), quoted in Paul Bew, *Ireland: the politics of enmity, 1789–2006* (Oxford, 2007), pp 144–5. 12 Olien, *Morpeth*, pp 152–3; Ó Tuathaigh, *Thomas Drummond*, pp 8–9.

overflowing solicitations from Irish members make them all rather ticklish matters'.[13] Securing official posts for Catholics was only half of the equation; at the same time, the administration looked to root out sectarian bias among Protestant officials. The key to this was the passing of the Irish Constabulary Act in 1836, which meant that appointments to the constabulary and magistracy were centralized; henceforth these positions were decided by Dublin Castle, who actively looked for able candidates with liberal views. Drummond oversaw the doubling in number of stipendiary magistrates, and by 1839 thirteen of these new appointments were Catholics and twenty-one Protestants. Membership of Orange Lodges or Ribbon societies was outlawed for those appointed to public office, and in 1837 the Orange magistrate Colonel Verner was sacked for having publicly toasted the Battle of the Diamond. This violent sectarian clash of 1795 in Armagh witnessed the death of dozens of Catholics and led to the founding of the Orange Order. Challenged over the dismissal, Morpeth was able to demonstrate misconduct on Verner's part.[14]

Mulgrave and Morpeth also worked hard to befriend O'Connell. They invited him to dinner, and Morpeth in particular went out of his way to entertain and receive nationalist MPs when they were in London, in marked contrast to the social ostracization they usually met with.[15] However, Morpeth was not present in Dublin to the same extent as Mulgrave and Drummond were, even though the chief secretary had an official residence in Phoenix Park. His job was to act as the link between Dublin and Westminster, to be answerable in the House of Commons and, crucially, to present draft legislation. Morpeth was a talented public speaker and an adroit political manager, but it was his personality – conciliatory, polite, never patronizing, self-effacing – that most assisted him and the administration in building good relations with Irish MPs.[16]

Morpeth never grew personally close to O'Connell, but he maintained a harmonious working relationship with him, and, in his letters to Mulgrave, he spoke of O'Connell with a mixture of bemusement, exasperation and

13 Morpeth to Mulgrave, 10 Mar., 21 May 1835, Mulgrave Castle MSS, M/437, 441.   14 The episode is recounted in Olien, *Morpeth*, pp 141–5; Richard Barry O'Brien, *Thomas Drummond, under-secretary in Ireland, 1835–40: life and letters* (London, 1889), pp 259–70.   15 Olien, *Morpeth*, pp 149–50. 16 For contemporary descriptions of Morpeth, see James Grant, *Random recollections of the House of Commons* (London, 1836), pp 114–15; G.H. Francis, *Orators of the age* (London, 1854), pp 160–6; *The English gentleman*, 10 Jan. 1836, p. 25. While often mocking his appearance, all were unanimous in their praise of his honest and upright character. See also John Tosh, 'Gentlemanly politeness and manly simplicity in Victorian England', *Transactions of the Royal Historical Society*, 12 (2002), 455–72.

concern.[17] O'Connell for his part warmly appreciated this acceptance into the political and social fold, whether in Dublin or London, even to the point of muting his demands for Repeal in the interests of this coalition. In 1837, during the debate on Ireland in the first parliament of Queen Victoria's reign, Mulgrave claimed that Repeal had been silenced:

> Three years ago the whole country rung with the cry of 'repeal'; where is that cry now? From one end of Ireland to another, the people are mute upon the subject of that once-popular demand – not a murmur is heard in any part of the kingdom; they are perfectly satisfied, perfectly content, with the English government.[18]

The Whig strategy of conciliation has been described as a means of 'killing Repeal with kindness'.[19] In 1840, Morpeth was to write, 'I am in hopes that the Repeal agitation is not making any real way', and passed on a report from the temperance leader, Fr Mathew, that 'the people out of Dublin do not really care about it'.[20] Just as Mulgrave was accused of being in thrall to O'Connell, so O'Connell and his followers were accused of abandoning their principles in the scramble for placement and patronage; their allegiance to the Whigs began to vitiate their reforming fervour. The journalist Daniel Madden was in no doubt that government patronage had 'succeeded to a considerable extent in pulverizing the Parliamentary Repeal Party': a fact made starkly apparent by the Repeal party's electoral collapse in 1841 when they slumped to just eighteen seats.[21] This hearts and minds strategy made up for the disappointing legislative achievements and it is largely on account of the personal style in which they conducted political business that Mulgrave, Morpeth and Drummond were remembered with such warmth. Thus, in his later years, Charles Gavan Duffy, one of the co-founders of the *Nation* newspaper, recalled Mulgrave's treatment of Catholics and Protestants 'on an

17 Olien, *Morpeth*, p. 151. In 1844, Morpeth followed O'Connell's trial and imprisonment for seditious conspiracy; on his release in September, he noted in his diary: 'Had to read O'Connell's long speech. I have seen too much of him ever to feel any intense interest for him', 11 Sept. 1844, Castle Howard Archives, J19/8/4. See Oliver MacDonagh, *The emancipationist, Daniel O'Connell, 1830–1847* (London, 1989), pp 244–52. 18 *Hansard*, xxxix, c.240, 247 (27 Nov. 1837). 19 Ó Tuathaigh, *Thomas Drummond*, p. 4; McDowell, *Public opinion and government policy in Ireland, 1801–1846* (London, 1952; repr. 1975), p. 172. 20 Morpeth to Mulgrave, 26 Sept. 1840, Mulgrave Castle MSS, V/364. 21 Daniel Madden, *Ireland and its rulers since 1829* (2nd ed., 3 vols, London, 1844), ii, 290–1. See also Angus Macintyre, *The Liberator: Daniel O'Connell and the Irish party, 1830–1847* (London, 1965), p. 65; MacDonagh sees O'Connell caught in 'a strange balance between political independence and collaboration': *The emancipist*, p. 190.

equal footing' during his tour of Ulster in 1836, which made a lasting impression on him; and he remembered Drummond as a similar exponent of even-handed 'fairplay'.[22]

But this troika of enlightened officialdom began to dissolve in 1839. In February, Mulgrave left for London having been moved to the cabinet post of secretary for the colonies and war. The *Freeman's Journal* reported on a meeting of Dublin citizens to decide on how to mark this departure. Mulgrave was eulogized by speaker after speaker as a 'kind and generous friend of our country, and the steady friend of even-handed justice' who had 'established imperishable claims to the eternal gratitude of the Irish people'. In an echo of Morpeth's experience some years earlier, Mulgrave was praised for enduring 'all manner of abuse and vituperation' heaped upon him; he had dared to act with justice 'in the teeth of prejudice, power and ascendancy'. His enlightened regime characterized by impartiality, justice and clemency contrasted starkly with the 'thick darkness' of previous periods, and his great achievement was to have torn down 'the wall of partition which divided Protestant from Catholic'. Lamenting this loss, the meeting took solace in the fact that his 'fellow labourers' remained behind. As long as Morpeth (also elevated to the cabinet at this time) and Drummond continued to manage the affairs of Ireland, the *Freeman's Journal* felt there was no cause for alarm.[23]

Mulgrave was succeeded by Lord Ebrington, under whose tenure Morpeth and Drummond were finally able to drive through reform of municipal corporations in 1840. In the same year, Drummond died. His death was a blow to Dublin Castle, where his industry and efficiency would be sorely missed, and his loss also occasioned generous tributes in the nationalist press. The *Morning Register* urged that 'we fix the memory of Mr Drummond in the nation's heart – the first English official, in the long centuries of our connection with England, so enshrined'.[24] And when the nationalist historian and biographer, Richard Barry O'Brien, came to write his life of Drummond in 1889, he claimed that he had 'ruled for the people and by the people'.[25]

And what of Morpeth? The loss of his West-Riding seat in July 1841 mirrored the collapse of Melbourne's government and the start of Peel's Tory

22 Quoted in O'Brien, *Thomas Drummond*, pp 378, 380; on the politics of justice for Ireland, see Peter Gray, *Famine, land and politics: British government and Irish society, 1843–50* (Dublin, 1999), pp 26–36. 23 *Freeman's Journal*, 15 Feb. 1839. In the same month, O'Connell wrote to Patrick Vincent Fitzpatrick: 'as a member of the cabinet we have Lord Morpeth. It is of the utmost use to Ireland ... it will throw the management of Irish affairs into his hands and they could not be in better': *Correspondence*, v, pp 215–17. 24 Quoted in O'Brien, *Thomas Drummond*, p. 389. 25 Ibid., p. 244. See also the qualifying view of Drummond in Gray, *The making of the Irish poor law*, p. 149, n. 51.

ministry. Morpeth vanished very quickly, leaving Ireland in September, and less than a month later he was crossing the Atlantic for a twelve-month tour of North America. His position on free trade and the Corn Laws had partly contributed to his defeat, and he had lost the support of the politically powerful non-conformists in the West Riding; but, in the eyes of some, he deserved to be punished because he had become too closely associated with O'Connell and his nationalist MPs (fig. 17).[26]

As with Mulgrave's departure, the impending loss of Morpeth prompted a series of meetings in Dublin. At the first of these, held at the Royal Exchange on 12 August to determine how to express public gratitude 'in any manner which would be most gratifying' to Morpeth, a committee was established under the chairmanship of the duke of Leinster with three secretaries. The account of the meeting echoed the similar gatherings held on the eve of Mulgrave's departure two years earlier, with some of the same individuals present: the Catholic baronet Sir Thomas Esmonde of Ballynastragh, Co. Wexford; the MP and barrister, Andrew Carew O'Dwyer; John Power, deputy lieutenant; the merchant Leland Crossthwaite; and Christopher Fitzsimon MP, barrister, and O'Connell's son-in-law. But the presiding force behind this meeting was O'Connell himself.

While the eulogies to Morpeth could almost be interchangeable with those made for Mulgrave, highlighting his labours in the 'cause of civil and religious liberties', there were significant differences as to how Irish gratitude was to be best marked on this occasion. More than once it was observed that any number of constituencies in Ireland would be made available for Morpeth to enable his speedy return to parliament if he so wished.[27] There was an undertone of anger at his ejection; Cecil Lawless spoke for many when he remarked 'we deplore the recent event which has deprived the country of the services of Lord Morpeth'. John Power first mooted the idea that the address 'be signed by every true friend of the country', and this was taken up by

26 For an account of the election and the reasons for Morpeth's defeat, see David Gent, 'Aristocratic Whig politics in early Victorian Yorkshire: Lord Morpeth and his world' (PhD, University of York, 2010), pp 138–49. 27 In fact, Morpeth was selected for Dublin city in January 1842 while he was travelling in North America. Despite O'Connell energetically canvassing on his behalf, he was defeated by William Henry Gregory. Morpeth was not favourably inclined to these efforts on his behalf: on receiving his mail from England, he noted in his American journal that all was well 'except the notion of starting me for Dublin', 27 Jan. 1842, Castle Howard Archives, J19/8. He had publicly declined such an offer in a letter to the *Dublin Monitor* as early as 16 August: *Leeds Mercury*, 28 Aug. 1841. It is worth remembering that O'Connell also lost his seat for Dublin in the 1841 election, but was quickly returned for Co. Cork: Patrick M. Geoghegan, *Liberator: the life and death of Daniel O'Connell, 1830–1847* (Dublin, 2010), p. 121.

ELECTORS
OF THE
WestRiding of Yorkshire

Your Fellow-Countrymen in South Devonshire, have done their Duty nobly, by Rejecting,

By a Majority of 628,
Lord John Russell
The Minion of O'CONNELL, the Supporter of Popery against Protestantism;

And if he again attempts to get into Parliament, it must be through the medium of one of those Close Boroughs, which he has been Denouncing all his Life.

Will you then be such Traitors to the Welfare of your Country, as not to follow their Glorious Example? No, you will not.—

The same Fate awaits LORD MORPETH.

You will send this NOMINEE of a Greedy Faction,—this TOOL of the Irish Roman Catholic Repealers, back to Castle Howard, to Spin Rhymes on the unhappy Fate of the Fat Bullocks which are fed on the " Fair Scenes of his Home."—YOU WILL REJECT THIS

Northern " Intruder,"
Who has not an Acre in the West Riding, and secure

A TRIUMPHANT MAJORITY
FOR YOUR FRIEND AND NEIGHBOUR,

John Stuart Wortley.
An ENEMY to POPERY & HUMBUG.

T. KEMP, PRINTER, HUDDERSFIELD.

17 The Tory election poster from the West-Riding by-election of May 1835, already dismissing Morpeth as a 'Tool of the Irish Roman Catholic Repealers'. In 1835, Morpeth defeated John Stuart Wortley by almost 3,000 votes but lost to him in 1841 (G.W. Tomlinson Collection, West Yorkshire Archive Service, Kirklees, KC174/84).

O'Connell who called for a 'multitude of signatures' to 'attest the united sentiments of the people of Ireland'. He envisaged a large document that could be handed to Morpeth, 'which he would, no doubt, preserve with pride for his remotest posterity'.

O'Connell's passionate speech was charged with political significances and rhetorical flourishes. He pointed out how chief secretaries 'were generally looked upon as common enemies of Ireland', but not so Morpeth. In praising him as 'honest and sincere', O'Connell reminded his audience that 'Ireland has but few friends, and those who take an interest in her welfare are in number small – indeed so much so, that it would require but a small bead roll upon which they might be counted'. O'Connell was already anticipating that the multitude of signatures shortly to be gathered would contrast hugely with this paucity of political friends. Similarly, Irish gratitude would show up English, or more specifically Yorkshire, ingratitude and hostility. Morpeth had been rejected because 'he was the enthusiastic friend of the civil and religious liberties of Ireland'. Had Morpeth chosen a different course, and not been defeated, then he would have 'stepped into the ranks of the enemies of Ireland'. O'Connell then likened Morpeth and the Howard family to the Geraldines in their service to Ireland, and astutely he cited the Howards' Catholic ancestry as proof of further affinity with the Irish. Morpeth might be a Protestant, but he was devout: 'What entitles him to more respect is the fact of his being a sincere religionist himself'. Furthermore, he was fair-minded: 'He is ready to give others the same liberty of opinions as that which he claims for himself'. Behind these tributes lay the implication that Morpeth was *one of us*.

O'Connell also cast an eye to Morpeth's political future, declaring 'with the most conscientious sincerity, that I believe he is destined to be one of the greatest and most leading men the British Empire contains'. In this, O'Connell was, as was his wont, picking up on a point voiced by someone else, in particular the mention earlier in the proceedings by John O'Neill, who had declared how he hoped yet to see Morpeth 'at the head of the state', at which point he would be 'sure Ireland would obtain her rights, and not till then'. These two comments hold an important clue as to why Morpeth was so feted. Many believed he would return and quite possibly as a future premier, in which case he would number among Ireland's most powerful advocates and friends.[28]

It is easy to be drawn in by the effusive and heady atmosphere in the Royal Exchange as reported in the *Freeman's Journal*. Political meetings often build up a momentum that impels people in a rapture of strong feelings. But this report, and the others that followed in both the English and the Irish press

28 *Freeman's Journal*, 13 Aug. 1841.

over the next four weeks, do withstand sceptical scrutiny. There is no doubt that Morpeth was held in high esteem and affection. The circumstances of his departure and his position in 1841 also explain why these valedictory outpourings were so different to those for Mulgrave and Drummond. Mulgrave was promoted to a cabinet post, and Drummond died suddenly. Morpeth, who had now served Ireland for longer than either of them (a total of six years), had not only developed a stronger reputation, but he had been the most closely identified with the legislation that had been passed. Richard Barry O'Brien likened the Dublin Castle administration to the command of a ship: the viceroy 'wears the insignia of command, but only signs the log'; the chief secretary 'is really the captain of the ship'; and the under secretary 'is the man at the wheel'. Insofar as this analogy holds true, it also accounts for why Morpeth was perceived as commander of the vessel.[29] But, as with politics in all ages, it was character that counted most, not forgetting that in the eyes of many it was inconceivable that a figure of such rectitude would not return to politics and quite probably ascend to the highest office. Looked at in this light, the Morpeth Roll takes on the status of a political gamble; it was a marker, something that could be cashed in at a future date.

The Irish preparations for the farewell presentation and banquet were also driven by a rivalry with Yorkshire. One day before the Royal Exchange meeting, the *Leeds Mercury* had reported how 'the people of Yorkshire are preparing to show their sense of the invaluable services of Lord Morpeth'; and it announced how subscriptions were being collected towards a 'splendid memorial', which might take the form of a 'gold vase, bearing a correct representation of the Emerald Isle in emeralds'.[30] By the end of August, the *Bradford Observer*, which had earlier reported O'Connell's Dublin speech in full, was pleased to announce that the Yorkshire testimonial was 'progressing most satisfactorily', and, what was more, it included the signatures of those who had voted against Morpeth. For many in Yorkshire, Morpeth's defeat was a calamity and an instance of 'base ingratitude', and their testimonial was a mark of 'regret' as well as a token of thanks. In conclusion, the paper was delighted to 'record the generous and heartfelt homage paid by the Irish people' to Morpeth, and considered itself to be 'engaged with them in a glorious rivalry'.[31]

---

29 Richard Barry O'Brien, *Dublin Castle and the Irish people* (Dublin, 1909), p. 33.   **30** *Leeds Mercury*, 14 Aug. 1841.   **31** *Bradford Observer*, 26 Aug. 1841; the charge of ingratitude was voiced by, among others, the Irish MP, Henry Grattan, in the *Freeman's Journal*, 6 Sept. 1841.

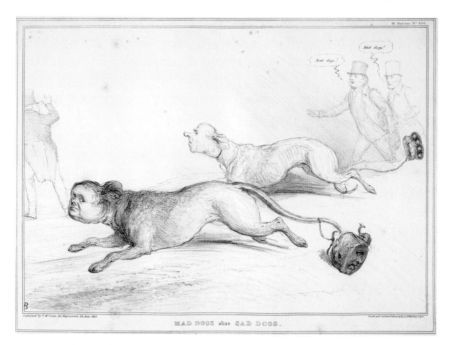

18 H.B., *Mad Dogs alias Sad Dogs*, no. 400, 26 June 1835 (the Castle Howard Collection).

But there is a further reason why Morpeth was so well known and liked. As chief secretary, he may have been less publicly visible in Ireland than the viceroy, especially since he was in London for much of the time, but that did not mean he escaped the attention of the satirical press. Like much of the political establishment of the day, Morpeth featured in the caricatures of the Dublin-born political cartoonist John Doyle, better known as 'H.B.'

A FAMILIAR FACE

In March 1836, *The Times* announced 'There are four persons who must live in perpetual horror of H.B.', and went on to identify these four as O'Connell, Lord John Russell, Morpeth and chancellor of the exchequer Thomas Spring Rice. 'On these four, the satirical artist has no mercy' *The Times* noted with approval. O'Connell, as is well known, was mercilessly lampooned in the English press, and *The Times* commended H.B. for exposing his 'vulgar swagger and cowardly cunning', and for portraying what a threat he was to the union. Among the satirical cartoons H.B. produced are depictions of him as

19 H.B., *A Gentle Warning*, no. 446, 26 July 1838 (the Castle Howard Collection).

a kangaroo, a comet, a genie, a serpent and Satan. In fact, H.B. devoted nearly a quarter of his nine hundred or so political sketches to the Irish M.P. But, if anything, *The Times* went on to commend H.B. for his caricatures of the other three figures in even more vitriolic terms, thundering at 'the prim conceit' of Russell, 'the feeble yet repulsive smirk' of Spring Rice, and 'the astounding whimsicality of countenance' of Morpeth.[32]

Morpeth appeared in more than sixty of H.B.'s political sketches. In many of them, he was a very minor presence, indeed in some he is hard to discern at all. In *Mad Dogs alias Sad Dogs*, Morpeth, or his face, is the tin can tied to O'Connell's tail (fig. 18). In others, Morpeth is a background figure, or one of a crowd; but in a good number he was more central to the satirical focus. The 'astounding whimsicality of countenance', noted by *The Times*, features in such cartoons as *A Gentle Warning*, where he stands sheepishly to one side, reprimanded by the duke of Wellington for parading too many Irish bills

32 *The Times*, 26 Mar. 1836; for H.B.'s depictions of O'Connell, see James N. McCord, 'The image of England: the cartoons of HB' in M.R. O'Connell (ed.), *Daniel O'Connell, political pioneer* (Dublin, 1991), pp 57–71.

TURNING THE TABLES.

20 H.B., *Turning the Tables*, no. 430, 25 March 1838 (the Castle Howard Collection).

(fig. 19). A similar slim figure is present in *Turning the Tables*, where the lord mayor and corporation are expelled from the room (fig. 20).

H.B. also emphasized Morpeth's boyish looks in a series of images that echoed written accounts of his appearance and demeanour. In *The Irish Tutor*, O'Connell is praising his diligent but docile pupils who include Melbourne, Russell, Palmerston and Morpeth (fig. 21). This boyishness was also seen as a mark of effeminacy; thus, in *The Modern Orpheus*, Morpeth is a bonneted matron clasping the Tithe Bill to his breast while charmed by O'Connell's lyre (fig. 22). He was not alone in being represented as a feminine figure; in April 1835, the diminutive Russell had appeared as a splendid Red Riding Hood encountering O'Connell the wolf (fig. 23). Later that year, Melbourne, Mulgrave and Morpeth were transformed into the witches who hail Macbeth in *A Travestie* (fig. 24). In congratulating H.B. on these cartoons, *The Times* noted his depiction of 'the Weird Brothers', but went on to qualify this: 'we suppose we must call them [such], though their weakness rather belongs to the gentler sex'.[33] This was a comment on the supposedly

33 *The Times*, 17 Nov. 1835.

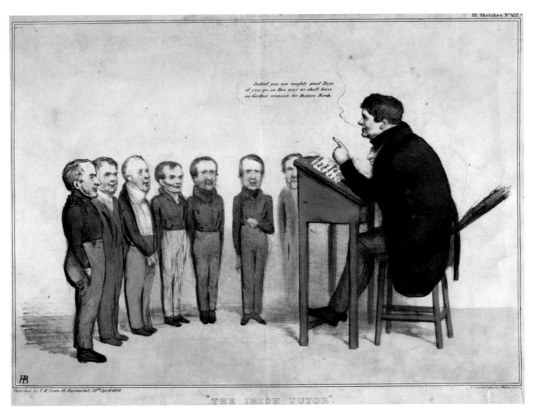

21 H.B., *The Irish Tutor*, no. 432, 29 April 1836 (the Castle Howard Collection).

22 H.B., *The Modern Orpheus, or The Progress of Civilisation: First Stage*, no. 401, 10 July 1838 (the Castle Howard Collection).

23 H.B., *Little Red Riding Hood's Meeting with the Wolf*, no. 385, 3 April 1835
(the Castle Howard Collection).

unmanly behaviour of Whigs in the face of O'Connell, who seemed to unsex them. O'Connell's apparent ability to disarm and emasculate his Whig allies is what spurred a number of H.B.'s cartoons. In *The Beggar's Petition*, the indigent O'Connell as Mother Ireland, with her large family, startles Morpeth

24 H.B., *A Travestie*, no. 416, 13 November 1835 (the Castle Howard Collection).

into dropping his own mendicity bill (fig. 25).[34] In *The New Lord Mayor of Dublin*, H.B. attacked the ambitions of O'Connell and his supporters, dismissing it as wishful thinking – the full title contains the cutting parenthesis '(That is to be)'. Under this regime, Morpeth and Mulgrave would be reduced to mere train-bearers following O'Connell, in whom power and pomp were now invested. In fact, this cartoon, dated 1835, came partially true in November 1841 when O'Connell did become lord mayor, but by that time Morpeth and Mulgrave were long absent from Dublin (fig. 26).[35]

H.B. often structured his sketches around a classical episode or a moment from literature or art, and enjoyed alluding to Dickens' novels. One of his finest sketches is *Oliver Introduced to the Respectable Old Gentleman*, where Mulgrave as the Artful Dodger ushers an innocent Morpeth into the presence of Fagin/O'Connell. Here, the satire is aimed at Mulgrave who has been co-opted into a team of ne'er-do-wells, while the shy, innocent Morpeth is in danger of being corrupted by the wily older man (fig. 27).

34 Gray, *The making of the Irish poor law*, p. 303.   35 MacDonagh, *The emancipationist*, pp 202–9.

25 H.B., *The Beggar's Petition*, 'this was the most unkindest cut of all', no. 631, 9 April 1840
(the Castle Howard Collection).

26 H.B., *The New Lord Mayor of Dublin (That is to be)*, no. 431, 25 March 1836
(the Castle Howard Collection).

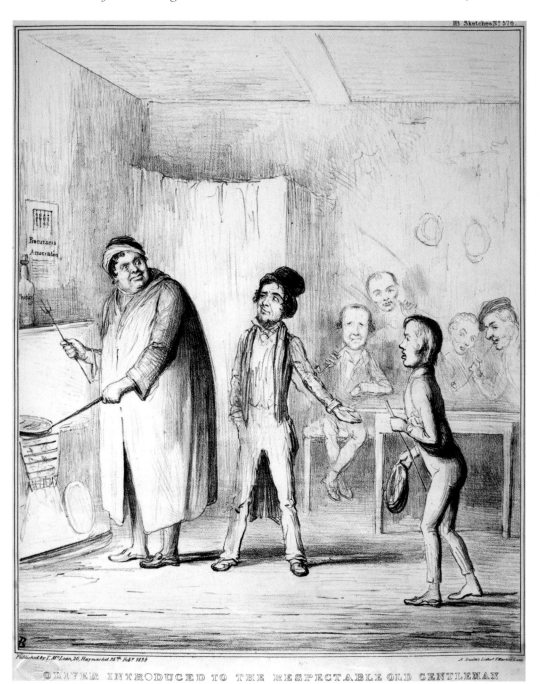

27 H.B., *Oliver Introduced to the Respectable Old Gentleman*, no. 576, 25 February 1839
(the Castle Howard Collection).

28 H.B., *A leaf out of Nicholas Nickleby with slight variations, Nicholas quits the company –*
Theatrical emotion of Mr Vincent Crummles, no. 582, 26 March 1839
(the Castle Howard Collection).

A month after this sketch appeared, H.B. published *A Leaf Out of Nicholas Nickleby with Slight Variations*, marking the moment in February 1839 when Mulgrave left Dublin (fig. 28). The print shows O'Connell smothering Mulgrave with a bear hug on Kingstown quayside before he embarks, while his son Morgan copies the action with an equally nonplussed Morpeth. O'Connell here is meant to be the slightly shambolic theatrical manager Vincent Crummles, whose troupe Nickleby joins during his wanderings in the early part of the novel; this moment comes from later on in the story, when Nickleby finally bids farewell to Crummles at Portsmouth, in a scene which for Dickens was in 'the highest style of melodrama'.[36] Crummles clasps Nickleby in what are described as a 'rapid succession of stage embraces, which as everybody knows, are performed by the embracer's laying his or her chin on the shoulder of the object of affection and looking over it'. H.B. enjoys exposing the sham affection displayed by O'Connell; it is nothing but a stage

36 *Nicholas Nickleby*, ch. xlviii. The novel was published in monthly parts between March 1838 and September 1839.

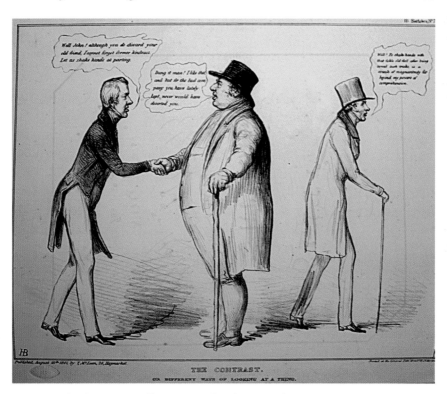

29 H.B., *The Contrast or Different Ways of Looking at a Thing,* no. 701, 19 August 1841 (the Castle Howard Collection).

hug designed to draw attention to the hugger rather than the recipient of the embrace, and this is reinforced by the figure of Lord Fortescue at the side, supplying the ironic comment 'What an affecting sight'.

But there is a second frame of action in the cartoon as Morgan O'Connell turns his head to make sure he is copying his father's theatrical pose correctly, an action that also allows his face to turn into view. In terms of the allusion to Dickens, O'Connell junior is meant to represent Master Crummles embracing Nickleby's companion Smike, who was the lame halfwit rescued from the infamous Dotheboys Hall school. There is indeed something wooden, if not actually gormless, about Morpeth's expression as he is embraced by the young O'Connell. H.B. is poking fun at Morpeth as much as he is O'Connell, reducing him to a simpleton.[37] The sketch appeared one

37 Smike turns out to be the illegitimate son of the wicked Ralph Nickleby. But, here, H.B. cannot be accused of casting doubt on Morpeth's parentage, because at this stage of the serialization of *Nicholas Nickleby* nobody (other than Dickens himself) knew of this secret family link, which would not be

month after Mulgrave's departure, and only a few weeks after this instalment of *Nicholas Nickleby*; it was, therefore, as with so many of H.B.'s cartoons, highly topical.

To a large extent, it was Morpeth's perceived capitulation to O'Connell that contributed to his electoral defeat in 1841, and, once out of office, he begins to disappear from H.B.'s political sketches. In *The Contrast*, issued in August of that year, Morpeth bids farewell to John Bull, who replies, 'Dang it man! I like thee and but for the bad company you have lately kept, never would have deserted you' (fig. 29). In *Breaking up of the Ice – A Sad Disaster*, Morpeth has vanished beneath the ice with only a hand and his 'West-Riding' hat visible as he sinks beneath the surface. O'Connell leans out ineffectually to try and save him, while grasping a signpost marked 'Dan[ge]rous', neatly capturing the political peril that had sunk Morpeth's career (fig. 30).

These cartoons were gently satirical, they lacked the spleen of earlier cartoonists such as James Gillray, and Morpeth took them in good humour, even colluding in some of them. In 1836, he wrote to Mulgrave:

> I have the honour of being associated with you in a new HB today, as train bearers to the new mayor of Dublin. Yours has no resemblance. I am unfairly used in another of the ejectment of the old corporations, as I had sent the suggestion for one section of the design myself.[38]

Morpeth's image was therefore a familiar one from the prevalence of his likeness in these cartoons, and because he was rarely, if ever, the butt of mordant humour or biting irony, they confirmed the popular impression of him as a gentleman, and a gentle man. In time, his placid, easy temperament was to count against him, and in 1839 Melbourne pointed to the short-comings of such political congeniality:

> The only fault Morpeth has is that he can deny no one anything that is asked and he will find this too great puerility and softness of disposition, altho' very amicable, a most serious inconvenience and impediment during his future political life.[39]

While briefly talked about as destined for the highest office, ultimately Morpeth was not ruthless enough to climb to the top of the political ladder.

revealed until the end of the novel. Within a few years, Dickens would know both Mulgrave and Morpeth in England.   38 Morpeth to Mulgrave, 25 Mar. 1836, Mulgrave Castle MSS, M/533.   39 Quoted in Olien, *Morpeth*, pp 205–6.

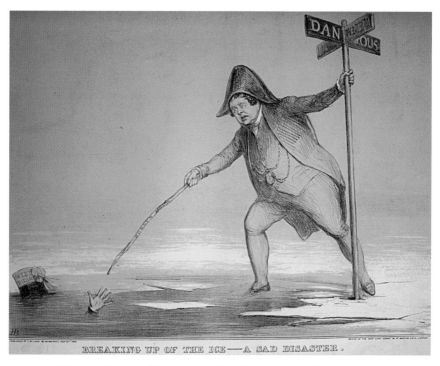

30 H.B., *Breaking up of the Ice: a Sad Disaster*, no. 716, 21 September 1841
(the Castle Howard Collection).

Indeed, it is hard to see how he could have done so without radically altering his personality.

FAREWELL TO MORPETH

The Morpeth testimonial was compiled in a remarkably short period of time, between the first meeting on 12 August and the presentation on 14 September. According to the *Freeman's Journal*, the presentation had the air of 'a great reform festival', with a thousand people crammed into the Royal Exchange to hear the duke of Leinster open with a summary of the signatures of peers, honourables, baronets, deputy lieutenants, magistrates, Roman Catholic bishops and a 'considerable number of Protestant and Dissenting clergymen of various denominations'. What turned the address from a vote of thanks from a select few into something genuinely demotic were the reported 257,000 names attached to it; with the duke adding 'a great number of signatures are still coming up from the country'.[40]

40 *Freeman's Journal*, 15 Sept. 1841.

WEEKLY MEETING OF THE REPEAL ASSOCIATION, CORN EXCHANGE, DUBLIN.

31 O'Connell speaking at a Repeal meeting in Dublin. His reliance on a network of grass-roots clubs, organizations and reading rooms greatly assisted him in his call for signatures for Morpeth's farewell address, *Illustrated London News*, 1843 (private collection).

In this respect, the compilation of the roll in just five weeks has to be seen as a triumph of organization and communication. While many could sign their names at offices in Dublin, the majority of the 652 sheets were delivered to the capital from the provinces. The mobilization of such support was undoubtedly due to O'Connell's public endorsement of such a document, and the fact that he and his supporters could call upon a sophisticated infrastructure to help produce the signatures. Repeal wardens, the activists working on behalf of the cause, were responsible for gathering signatures in various localities, as were parish priests.[41] The long tradition of Catholic assemblies, so many of them the brainchild of O'Connell, and stretching back to the founding of the Catholic Association in 1823, had established an

41 *Freeman's Journal*, 8, 9 Sept. 1841. Repeal wardens have been described as 'O'Connell's police': Stewart J. Brown, *Providence and empire: religion, politics and society in the United Kingdom* (Harlow, 2008), p. 124.

efficient network for political news to flow back and forth between the capital and the country. Social clubs, reading rooms, constituency clubs and voluntary organizations helped circulate political news and stimulate discussion. This tradition of engagement at grass-roots level, aided by politically active clergy, undoubtedly helped in the swift compiling of signatures (fig. 31).[42] The presence of Charles Bianconi's name early on in the roll also explains why such support could be mobilized so rapidly. There can be little doubt that his cars will have delivered sheets to Dublin. His pioneering transport network, begun in 1815, had grown to the point that by 'the early 1840s only a few of the more remote parts of Ireland were more than ten miles from some form of public transport'.[43] By comparison, the Yorkshire testimonial was compiled at a more leisurely pace; it did not need to be presented with the same degree of urgency since Morpeth was returning home to Castle Howard.

On receiving the roll in Dublin, Morpeth, clearly overcome at the scale of this farewell, responded with characteristic grace. He obliged O'Connell by agreeing that the testimonial was 'the richest heirloom I could bequeath to the name I bear', and bade his farewell to associates, friends and the Irish people with stoical dignity.[44] The address to which all the signatures were appended specified how it been organized by the Reformers of Ireland, and it was formulated in part as a statement of post-Emancipation appreciation:

> We hold in our grateful remembrance the devotedness with which, in early life – in those dark days of bondage, when a vast majority of our fellow countrymen were oppressed for conscience sake, – Your Lordship ranged yourself with the friends of Ireland; And we have marked the earnestness with which Your Lordship has ever since essayed to impart life and spirit to the cold form of civil and religious enfranchisement, which you and others had created.

The language captured an emotional bond between Morpeth and those whom he had helped to deliver from darkness; the metaphor of Morpeth bringing life and spirit to a cold form invoked the idea of animism and

42 See Macintyre, *The liberator*, pp 6–7, 78–80, 83–4, 89–90, 113; Foster, *Modern Ireland*, 298, 307–9; Róisín Higgins, 'The *Nation* reading rooms' in James H. Murphy (ed.), *The Oxford history of the Irish book*, iv: *The Irish book in English, 1800–1891* (Oxford, 2011), pp 262–73; Naoki Sakiyama, 'Dublin merchants and the Irish repeal movement of the 1840s', *Journal of International Economic Studies*, 24 (2010), 40–2. 43 Thomas P. O'Neill, 'Bianconi and his cars' in Kevin B. Nowlan (ed.), *Travel and transport in Ireland* (Dublin, 1973), p. 86; see also M. O'C. Bianconi and S.J. Watson, *Bianconi, king of the Irish roads* (Dublin, 1962). 44 *Freeman's Journal*, 15 Sept. 1841.

creation. However, while emancipation had at last grown to successful maturity, the same could not be said for the cause of Repeal. In 1833, at a dinner in Cork, Fergus O'Connor had likened O'Connell's movement to Frankenstein's monster, a creature nurtured for decades before its maker chose to turn it loose upon the world 'full of maturity, and perfect in all its parts'.[45] The irony is that much of Morpeth's legislation from the 1830s had been imperfect; it was a hybrid or compromise designed to appease political opponents on the left or the right. It was far from mature and perfect in its parliamentary creation; and Repeal, which had been studiously ignored by the Whigs, remained cold and inert, even more so after the disappointing election results of 1841. Historians seem divided in their assessment of the legislative achievements of the 1830s, and it is as easy to overstate the successes as it is to belittle them. Perhaps the most significant fact is that such a volume of measures actually reached the statute book – something unthinkable under previous administrations and before emancipation.[46] As Patrick Cosgrove has argued, the Morpeth Roll was a political document, gesturing to the politics of mass agitation in which size, scale or volume counted for much. Monster meetings with huge petitions were one of the ways in which those excluded from power articulated their grievances. The testimonial could not be entirely ignored by Peel's administration. It was a graphic reminder of O'Connell's ability to mobilize opinion and support: signatures that appeared as a vote of thanks at one moment might very well be channelled in the direction of mass opposition on another occasion. The contrast with the Yorkshire testimonial is instructive of the two different political spheres inhabited by Morpeth. He received two farewells from his West-Riding constituents, a testimonial roll similar to the Dublin document, and a handsome wine cooler fashioned out of bog oak and silver gilt. This was blazoned with twenty-six small plaques naming the towns in his constituency, and the inscription specified the 'deep regret for the loss of his valuable services' felt by his friends and supporters (fig. 32). It was a civic expression of gratitude, whereas the Irish scroll was a testimony to individualism and the power of mass response.

The random way in which the Irish sheets have been attached together with no apparent sequence or hierarchy, and with many sheets carrying little

45 *Freeman's Journal*, 7 Nov. 1833; in the same week, the Theatre Royal in Dublin staged the first performance of the 'melo-dramatic spectacle, Frankenstein or the Man-Monster'. O'Connell would be depicted as a monster by H.B., and the first cartoon depicting Irishmen as Frankenstein's deformed creature appeared in *Punch* in 1843.   46 For a discussion of the cautious and popular dimensions to Whig policy, see Gearóid Ó Tuathaigh, *Ireland before the Famine* (Dublin, 1972), pp 162–4; and his *Thomas Drummond*, pp 18–20.

32 The wine cooler made from bog oak and silver gilt, presented to Morpeth by his West-Riding friends and supporters, and blazoned with the names of twenty-six towns (the Castle Howard Collection).

or no identification of location, is also in marked contrast to the Yorkshire scroll, where each sheet is headed by voting district and ward. Perhaps it is no coincidence that the most carefully tallied sheets in the Irish roll come from parishes in Ulster with identifying labels and totals of names recorded. The Yorkshire address rehearses the familiar valedictory sentiments of esteem and gratitude, as well as the wish that Morpeth will one day return to politics and to the West Riding in particular. In his departing speech, Morpeth had made it clear that he would never 'accept a mission from any other constituent body', which is why he refused offers of an Irish seat. The tone is more formal, opening with a reflection on the moment of its composition; appropriately, this is well after the electoral 'tumult', when 'delusion' had triumphed at the hands of those who voted him out of office:

> ... the struggle is now over; the excitement has died away; party animosities are forgotten in friendly intercourse; and the time, as we conceive, has arrived, when we may, with offence to no one, record in this solemn and deliberate manner, our esteem, our admiration and our regret (fig. 33)

The Yorkshire roll has only recently been investigated and it is clear that, in their rivalry with Ireland, Yorkshire came second. The Yorkshire testimonial measures just over 120 metres and contains approximaelty 50,000 signatures. But this address is in many ways eclipsed by the wine cooler, reputed to have cost one thousand guineas; as a spectacular example of the decorative arts, it is more easily viewed and comprehended than a gigantic roll of paper, which, unlike its Irish counterpart, was not mounted on a bobbin.[47] Quite what Morpeth thought of these gifts privately is not known; he only began keeping a journal at the start of his American tour in the autumn of 1841.

The farewell was no doubt heartfelt on all sides, but it would be a mistake to think that Morpeth had been in perfect harmony with Irish politicians. He remained opposed to Repeal, he did not always agree with O'Connell, and at times outmanoeuvred him in parliament. In his rather schematic survey of Dublin Castle officials, whom he listed as either 'in sympathy' or 'out of sympathy' with the people, Richard Barry O'Brien grouped Morpeth as one of the few chief secretaries favourable to Ireland; however, when reviewing the viceroys of the nineteenth century, he placed Carlisle (as he then was) among the majority who were out of sympathy with the people.[48]

THE RETURN AS CARLISLE

In 1846, Morpeth successfully returned to politics, representing the West Riding in Lord Russell's ministry.[49] He remained in the House of Commons until his elevation to the Lords as seventh earl of Carlisle in 1848, and in 1855 Lord Palmerston appointed him viceroy of Ireland, a post he occupied until 1864, save for an eighteen-month hiatus in 1858–9 when Palmerston's ministry was replaced by that of Lord Derby (fig. 34). Ill health caused him to leave Ireland in October 1864, and he returned to Castle Howard, where he died two months later. This second term of office in Ireland, between 1855 and 1864, is more richly documented, not least of all through his diaries, and more than one hundred volumes of correspondence, a large proportion of which relates to Irish matters (fig. 35). The objects of material

47 The wine cooler made by Wilkinson of Leeds was described in the *Illustrated London News*, 3 Feb. 1844. It finally reached Castle Howard in May 1844. Morpeth recorded the moment but was silent about the Yorkshire testimonial: diary, 13–14 May 1844, Castle Howard Archives, J19/8/3.   48 O'Connell fell out with Morpeth over the Grocer's Spirit Licences Bill in 1838, accusing him of treachery: *Correspondence*, vi, pp 164–9; O'Brien, *Dublin Castle*, pp 10–17.   49 For Morpeth's later political career, see Olien, *Morpeth*, chs 6, 8, 9; Gent, 'Aristocratic Whig politics', ch. 4.

33 The opening address to Morpeth from his West-Riding constituents, 1841 (Castle Howard Archives).

To Lord Viscount Morpeth

My Lord

If we had given utterance to our feelings at the moment when the tie which had so long bound you to us was severed, our professions of attachment and concern might have been confounded with the mass of panegyric and invective which a general election never fails to produce; but the struggle is now over; the excitement has died away; party animosities are forgotten in friendly intercourse; and the time, as we conceive, has arrived, when we may, with offence to no one, record in this solemn and deliberate manner, our esteem, our admiration, and our regret.

It would ill become us to condole with your Lordship on the late change in the representation of this Riding, or on the still more important change which has taken place in the Government of the country:— It is impossible, we are well assured, that any such reverse should have found you unprepared. When you engaged in the tumult of party and the cares of government, you were not ignorant of the fate which has, in every age, attended those who have laboured for the happiness of nations. You well know how frequently the prejudices and partial interests which exist in every large community, are opposed to those who would serve it; and to what exertions and sacrifices mankind has been indebted for the victories of liberty, and of truth.

You have, moreover, in this great turn of fortune, whatever support can be derived from the resources of a youthful and highly cultivated mind; from the voice of an approving conscience; from the blessings of great masses of the people, both in Great Britain and in Ireland; from the regard of friends whose esteem and affection are fixed, not only on the minister, but also on the man; from the testimony borne even by opponents, to your ability, your humanity and your honour; and above all, from the deep though unaffected tone of your religious feelings. To you, therefore, we do not presume to offer personal condolence, but we must be permitted to express our deep concern at the manner in which the connexion between you and your late constituents has terminated.

The West Riding has ill performed its part. The place of the West Riding was not in the ranks of monopoly. Here, if nowhere else, should have been found, combined with the power to promote, the intelligence to comprehend, and the spirit to maintain, the great principles of commercial freedom:— Here, if nowhere else, it should have been known, how much the activity of manufactures, and the enterprise of trade, contribute to the welfare of the proprietors and cultivators of the soil; and here we might have expected a practical manifestation of that knowledge. But delusion has triumphed, and we have only by this public act, to disclaim our participation in that delusion, and to avow our regret that others have given their support, a support which, we cannot doubt, they will ere long see reason to deplore, to a system, alike hostile to the extension of our foreign commerce, and to the other great interests of the British Empire, and which, by counteracting the beneficent dispensations of providence, is especially incompatible with the prosperity of this district.

There is one period in which your Lordship will perhaps permit us to offer our counsel. On the day when with grace, gentleness, and dignity, such as extorted admiration, even from political opponents, you took your leave of us, we heard from you words, which we trust are to be considered, only as the expression of a transient feeling; which, though natural at such a time, to such a mind, will yield on reflection, to the sense of public duty. You declared that, having so long sat in parliament, as the representative of this great Riding, you were then unwilling to accept a mission from any other constituent body. The day, we trust, will arrive, when our dearest interests will again be confided to your immediate care; but your country cannot spare you even till that day. The united Empire, suffering under a legislation which turns her most profitable customers against their will, into her most formidable competitors, has a claim to your services.

It will be assured, highly gratify us to learn, that those talents and virtues which the greatest constituent body in the empire has rejected, have been justly appreciated and honored elsewhere.

And now, my Lord, with all gratitude for your long, your faithful, your ill-requited services, with all respect for your principles and talents, and with all good wishes for your happiness, and for the happiness of your noble house, we, for the present, bid you farewell.

G. W. Fitzwilliam
Fitzwilliam
Wood
W. Beauford
John Evelyn Denison

Scarborough
Howard   Charles Wood
Geo Wile Talbemele
W. C. Weies Esq

Newton Milton
Withers
Weston
James B. Garforth

G. W. Fitzwilliam
Edw Rowson
W. R. C. Stansfield
W. B. Wrightson
Landon Briggs

George John Sargeanton
William Smith
W. Henry Leatham
Jos Heminster
J. G. Smyth
Edw Baines

Will Brook
Wm Leatham
D. Maude
Fred W. Wilson
Francis Maude
Peter Williams

Wm Wood
John Smeatham
Geo Goodman
Peter Heyward
Thos W. Tottie
Henry B. Symons
Thomas Banff

F. H. Fawkes
H. Hatfield
Charles W. Crossfield
Fred Greenwood
John W. Tottie
Jn Hope Shaw

Townships of Leeds
(Mill Hill Ward)
J. C. Clapham
George Rawnsley
Wm Bishop
Edw Baines Jn
Wjohn Cameron

Leeds Polling District.

Robt Robinson
Thomas Beale
Thomas Nunneley
Sam Hackett

Geo W. Bischoff
the Richd Townend
J. Patterson
Jno Smith

R. E. Payne
John Heaton
Wm Harrington
Wesley Tomlinson
W. L. Wham

34 John Partridge, *George Howard, seventh earl of Carlisle*, c.1850, oil on canvas
(the Naworth Castle Collection).

culture associated with him from this period are just as prolific. He spent
much of his time as viceroy engaged in ceremonial duties, laying countless
foundation stones, digging sods and making speeches. A collection of silver
trowels, spades and wheelbarrows testifies to these civic occasions and
includes: the Tralee/Killarney Railway (1855); the Limerick Sailors' Home
(1856); the Wexford Crimea Memorial (1857); St Patrick's Bridge, Cork
(1859); the Queenstown branch of the Cork/Youghal Railway (1859); the
Molyneux Asylum for the Blind, Dublin (1860); the Dublin Corporation
Waterworks reservoir at Stillorgan (1862); and the Dublin Concert and
Exhibition buildings (1863) (fig. 36). On two of these occasions, Carlisle was
captured in photographs (figs 37, 38). In 1858, at the end of his first term as
viceroy, Carlisle was presented with a silver and yew wood casket in simulated

35 The viceregal lodge, *c.*1860, one of a series of images in Carlisle's album illustrating his time as viceroy between 1855 and 1864 (the Castle Howard Collection).

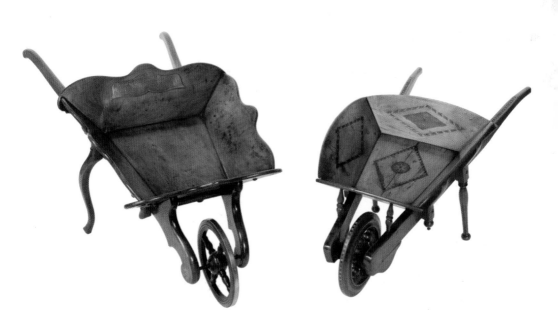

36 Two ceremonial wheelbarrows presented to Carlisle when he was viceroy, on the opening of the Queenstown branch of the Cork/Youghal Railway in 1859 (*left*) and the Tralee/Killarney Railway in 1855 (*right*) (the Castle Howard Collection).

37 Carlisle laying the foundation of the Carlisle Tower at Lismore Castle, Co. Cork, the
Irish home of his uncle, the sixth duke of Devonshire, on 24 September 1855
(the Castle Howard Collection).

basketwork from the ladies of the viceregal court in thanks for his hospitality.
Incised on the silver clasp are the names of 129 ladies. The knack of acquiring
handsome farewell gifts seems never to have deserted Carlisle (figs 39, 40).[50]

In 1857, he was presented with a volume containing photographs of 110
convicts by John Lentaigne, inspector general of prisons (figs 41, 42). Carlisle
was not an official who favoured a harsh penal system; in Yorkshire, he
pioneered a Reform School on the Castle Howard estate – he was a reformer
in penal matters as well as in religious, educational and political ones. He
regularly visited prisons and reformatories in London and Dublin, and would
therefore have endorsed the Latin epigraph from Horace on the title page,
which translates as 'No one is so savage that they cannot be tamed', and was
the Mountjoy Prison motto. Lentaigne, who was a physician by training,
seems also to have been a pioneer in the use of photography for criminal
identification, but it is clear that these images are intended not only to record

---

50 This reaches its climax with the 110ft granite commemorative column erected posthumously by
public subscription in 1869–70 on the Castle Howard estate, designed by Frederick Pepys Cockerell.

38 Carlisle laying the foundation stone of Edwin Thomas Willis' Crimea monument at Ferrycarrig, Co. Wexford, in October 1857 (the Castle Howard Collection).

but to classify too. The fashionable sciences of phrenology and physiognomy lie behind this exercise, the former a subject in which Carlisle had shown interest earlier in his life. The identities and case histories of the convicts are contained in a separate notebook; in the album, their appearance, and occasionally their prison number, are all that individualize them, and one has to look elsewhere for a key to who they were.[51] Carlisle often exercised clemency when reviewing capital cases, and in 1858 he refused to sanction the use of straitjackets for prisoners until he had tried one on for himself.[52] In an extraordinary episode on St Patrick's Day in 1864, he recorded in his diary that, while standing on the balcony at Dublin Castle and throwing down sponge biscuits to the crowd below (as was apparently the custom), a youth threw one back at the party, and was locked in the cells by constables. Carlisle intervened and had the boy released immediately (fig. 43).[53] These and other

51 Castle Howard Archives, J19/11/12. For Lentaigne, see *DIB*, v, pp 453–4.   52 'I walked to Mountjoy Prison & made Mr Wetherell, the governor, put me into a strait waistcoat, before I consent to give authority for its use': diary, 5 Feb. 1856, Castle Howard Archives, J19/8/36.   53 'I heard in the afternoon he was committed for a month's imprisonment, I very soon had him out again': diary, 17 Mar.

39 The silver and yew wood chest made by J. Thackery of Dublin, and presented to
Carlisle in October 1858, by the ladies of the viceregal court, thanking him for
his hospitality (the Castle Howard Collection).

episodes not only gainsay the stereotypical image of the flinty-hearted British
official in Ireland, but show how his popularity in Ireland continued to grow
during his second period of office.

The age of mechanical reproduction meant that Carlisle acquired other
photographic records, including an album of life at the viceregal lodge,
illustrating members of his court. Also recorded are images of Carlisle's own
cricket team; it was a sport he was passionate about and did much to promote
in Ireland. When one reads in his diaries of the endless games of cricket,
croquet and whist he played in Dublin, and how seriously he viewed these
pastimes, one can understand how some have criticized his time as viceroy as
little more than ineffectual flummery and frivolous ornamentalism (fig. 44).[54]

1864, Castle Howard Archives, J19/8/40.   **54** K. Theodore Hoppen, 'A question none could answer:
"what was the viceroyalty for?", 1800–1921' in Gray (ed.), *Irish lord lieutenancy*, p. 135.

40 Incised on the silver clasp are the names of 129 ladies (the Castle Howard Collection).

Representations of Carlisle abound too; he was sculpted three times by the Dublin-born sculptor John Foley, all posthumously. There is a marble bust at Castle Howard (and a second version in Morpeth Town Hall, Northumberland); a lead statue near Carlisle in Cumbria with Carlisle in historical costume; and a full-length figure that used to stand in Phoenix Park until damaged in a bomb attack in 1958 and subsequently removed (figs 45, 46).[55]

55 Paula Murphy, *Nineteenth-century Irish sculpture: native genius reaffirmed* (New Haven, CT, and London, 2010), pp 227–8. See also Ingrid Roscoe (ed.), *A biographical dictionary of sculptors in Britain, 1660–1851* (New Haven, CT, and London, 2009), pp 476–83.

Photographs

of

One Hundred and Ten of the more Serious Offenders,

confined under Penal and Reformatory Discipline,

in Mountjoy Government Cellular Prison, Dublin.

"Nemo adeo ferus est, ut non mitescere possit."

Horatii Epist. I ad Mecenatem.

August 1857

John Lentaigne

41 The title page to the album of convicts at Mountjoy Prison, presented to Carlisle in 1857 by John Lentaigne (the Castle Howard Collection).

42 Each page of the Mountjoy album contains a pair of photographs. The case histories of each prisoner were recorded in a separate notebook (the Castle Howard Collection).

43 Carlisle and party on the balcony of Dublin Castle, St Patrick's Day 1864. When a young boy threw a biscuit at them from the crowd he was apprehended by constables, but Carlisle intervened and had him released from the cells within hours (the Castle Howard Collection).

In May 1856, he sat to the artist Catterson Smith for his official portrait as viceroy. The painting took more than a year to complete and required multiple sittings, which tested Carlisle's patience.[56] The gestation for this picture says something about either Smith's artistic abilities or Carlisle's physique. The custom was for the viceroy to commission a portrait and then present it to Dublin Castle, but of the twenty-eight portraits in this series that used to hang in the castle, only seventeen remain today, mostly on display in the gallery. A number were destroyed in a fire in 1941 and five appear to have been sold in the twentieth century. Smith's portrait has disappeared.[57] He also followed the rage for *cartes-de-visite*, which had burst upon fashionable society in the 1850s. He visited Thomas Cranfield's studio in Grafton Street, where he was captured in a relaxed attitude, clearly having put on weight

56 Diary, 5 May 1856; by 26 September 1857 he had sat for the nineteenth time: Castle Howard Archives, J19/8/34–5. **57** Róisín Kennedy, *Dublin Castle art: the historical and contemporary collection* (Dublin, 1999), pp 30–48.

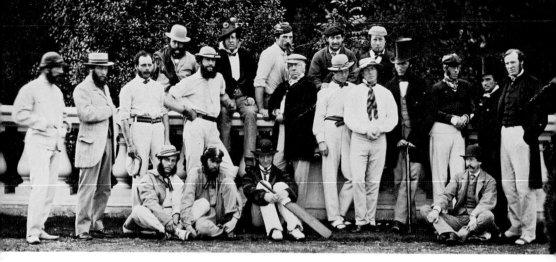

44 The viceregal lodge cricket team. It was a sport Carlisle was passionate about and he would insist on scoring the matches (the Castle Howard Collection).

45 John Foley, bust of George Howard, seventh earl of Carlisle, 1871, marble (the Castle Howard Collection).

46 (*opposite page*) John Foley, statue of George Howard, seventh earl of Carlisle, 1870, Brampton, Cumbria, bronze.

ERECTED
BY THE PEOPLE OF CUMBERLAND
TO COMMEMORATE
THE PUBLIC SERVICES AND PERSONAL WORTH OF
GEORGE WILLIAM FREDERICK HOWARD,
SEVENTH EARL OF CARLISLE, K.G.
BORN APRIL 18, 1802. DIED DECEMBER 5, 1864.

47 Thomas Cranfield, *carte-de-visite* of George Howard, seventh earl of Carlisle, c.1860 (the Castle Howard Collection).

(fig. 47). During these years, his image begins to metamorphose, unsurprisingly, into one of an elder statesman, and his diaries record repeated visits to photographic studios. At Symington's in Dublin, he recorded in 1858 how 'my ugliness was stereotyped three times'; at Mansfield's studio in Grafton Street, he sat for three abortive pictures: 'I was told I moved each time', he commented. And in 1864, only months before he retired, he sat to Charles Scott at his premises in Upper Sackville Street for a coloured photograph. In this composition, he leans against a pillar in a sober pose, finely dressed and exuding an air of gravitas, his seniority enhanced by fashionable but not excessive side-whiskers (fig. 48).[58]

58 Diary, 30 May 1854; 13 May 1858; 26 Feb., 2 Apr., 6 Sept. 1860; 9 Aug. 1861; 6 Mar. 1862; 15 Feb. 1864, Castle Howard Archives, J19/8/32, 36, 37, 39.

48 C.R. Scott, coloured photograph of George Howard, seventh earl of Carlisle, 1864 (the Castle Howard Collection).

Finally, and most intriguingly, there is a portrait of Carlisle and his retinue on the steps of the viceregal lodge (fig. 49). It was begun in 1856 by the portraitist Nicholas Crowley but, following his sudden death, it was completed by Michael Angelo Hayes.[59] The portrait returned to Castle Howard and in the 1870s his younger brother Edward Howard asked a local Yorkshire artist, John Robert

59 Diary, 18, 29 Feb. 1856; 27 Mar. 1857, Castle Howard Archives, J19/8/34, 35.

49 Nicholas Crowley and Michael Angelo Hayes, *The seventh earl of Carlisle as viceroy with his retinue on the steps of the viceregal lodge*, 1856–7, oil on canvas. This is the version of the picture today after restoring it to as near to the original composition as possible (the Castle Howard Collection).

Milner, to remove eight figures from the composition, and alter Carlisle's features and the background scenery (fig. 50).[60] An undated letter naming the unfortunate individuals survives and points to the fact that somebody was able to recognize the figures in question, either by their likeness or from a key (now lost) to the picture (fig. 51). The motive for their erasure remains a mystery, but it is unlikely to have been for aesthetic reasons. Over the years, the figures began to ghost through the over-paint and in the 1990s the decision was taken to try and restore the picture to as close to its original state

---

60 Undated memorandum signed by John Duthie, house steward at Castle Howard, Castle Howard Archives, W 3 / 1. Milner of Malton began his career as an artist, but by the 1860s he had also become a photographer.

50 The viceregal portrait after Milner had made the alterations demanded by Edward Howard. Eight individuals have been removed, the background scenery altered, and Carlisle's features dramatically changed (the Castle Howard Collection).

as possible. Seven of the figures were recovered; the eighth had been scratched out too severely to permit recovery (fig. 52). The painting on show today is therefore something of a hybrid, a near approximation of what was the finished piece in 1857.

It is difficult to match the names to the recovered faces with any certainty, notwithstanding the fact that Carlisle's photograph album has pictures of some of these figures. The painted features of surgeon Dr Hatchell, and vice chamberlain Henry Leeson are too imprecise to allow a confident identification (figs 53, 54). A further enigma is in how the artist failed to erase at least one of the named figures. Walter Creyke, whose name at the top of the list appears to have been added at a different stage, if the fainter ink is anything to go by, survived this painterly cull. Creyke is much easier to identify from his photograph, distinguished as he is by a fine beard and curly

51 The undated memorandum to John Milner signed by John Duthie, house steward at Castle Howard, conveying instructions from Edward Howard, Lord Lanerton, to remove eight figures from the portrait (Castle Howard Archives).

hair with centre parting, and his hirsute head remained unscathed in the background of the picture (figs 55, 56). This, of course, means that somebody else was mistaken for Creyke.

As if this was not enough, the other major oddity is how Carlisle's own features were altered. In the amended portrait, his face acquired a ghastly appearance – he looks grey, unwell and ancient (figs 57, 58).[61] It was only in the course of the restoration that it became apparent how these elements had

61 As Carlisle aged, he became increasingly unwell. He seems to have been prone to high blood pressure, dizziness, numbness and intermittent loss of voice, and his features showed signs of the passage of time, but not to the extent that they appear in the amended portrait.

a

b

c

52a/b/c Details showing the gradual recovery of the face of the single woman named in the letter as Miss Tighe (the Castle Howard Collection).

53 Dr Hatchell, surgeon in ordinary at the viceregal court (the Castle Howard Collection).

54 Henry Leeson, Carlisle's vice chamberlain (the Castle Howard Collection).

55 Walter Creyke, one of Carlisle's private secretaries and mainstay of the viceregal cricket team (the Castle Howard Collection).

56 Walter Creyke as he appears in the viceregal portrait; he escaped erasure when Milner mistook somebody else for him (the Castle Howard Collection).

been introduced to obscure a more youthful physiognomy (at the time of the portrait in 1856–7, Carlisle was in his early fifties). This transformation is utterly mystifying, it changes the moment of the painting in a radical way, literally obliterating people from view in a way we normally associate with Stalin's actions towards his Bolshevik colleagues. By this logic, Milner's alterations mean that certain people were not deemed to have been present in 1856–7, and were no longer recognized as part of the viceregal household. Perhaps the strangest part of this intervention is how an older Carlisle has been inserted into this composition when, as we have seen, his features were far from haggard. Young or old, healthy or unwell, fresh or aged, it becomes difficult to decide on which is the real Carlisle. Twenty years or so after this moment at Castle Howard, the world would be introduced to a character whose painted face aged secretly on a canvas in an attic while his real physiognomy remained eternally fresh and beautiful, in Oscar Wilde's *Picture of Dorian Grey* (1891). The reason for Edward Howard's drastic intervention with his brother's portrait remains obscure, but it seems likely that scandal, either real or feared, lies at the heart of this perplexing picture.

57 Detail of Carlisle's face with the haggard features introduced by Milner (the Castle Howard Collection).

58 Detail of Carlisle's fresher appearance in the restored version of the portrait; this is nearer to how he looked in 1856 (the Castle Howard Collection).

Morpeth's relationship with Ireland spanned five decades, from when he first attended the emancipation dinner in 1828 until his departure in 1864. Only now is the extent of his involvement becoming truly apparent, as is the wealth of material associated with him. He has inevitably been overshadowed by his more famous and influential political contemporaries, Melbourne Russell, Peel, Palmerston to name but a few. This does not mean he is a man devoid of interest. His diaries may not be filled with political gravitas or crackling gossip, nor do they contain strenuous intellectual reflection, nevertheless they are an invaluable source of information on the man and his times, in part because he moved through so many sections of society – in England, Ireland, Europe and North America. He is rather like a star in the outer reaches of the universe: recognizable and slightly obscure, but moving among a constellation of larger, brighter bodies, while touching them or being touched by them. For a brief moment in Ireland in the summer of 1841 Morpeth's star burned brightest, just as it was crashing to earth.

Investigating the Morpeth Roll

PAUL HOARY

T HE GENERAL ELECTION OF 1841 ended on 22 July and fifty-four days
later, on 14 September, Lord Morpeth was presented with a farewell
address reportedly containing 257,000 signatures. The testimonial took the
form of hundreds of sheets of signed paper wrapped around a spool or
bobbin, which rests inside a bespoke military chest and sits on two u-shaped
brass brackets attached to the insides of the box, thus enabling the bobbin to
rotate. The Morpeth Roll is therefore a mechanical object in addition to
being a most impressive document. The first two sheets that emerge contain
the address to Lord Morpeth signed by the 'Reformers of Ireland'. These are
followed by more than six hundred sheets containing a 'multitude' of
signatures.[1] The roll subsequently travelled to Morpeth's ancestral home of
Castle Howard in North Yorkshire, where it is generally believed it
languished in obscurity until its recent rediscovery.

On loan from Castle Howard, the roll arrived in Maynooth in 2010 for
research and conservation, and was delivered to the Russell Library. By
chance, the library was experienced in displaying and working with objects of
unusual size and shape, having exhibited the manuscript of Jack Kerouac's
novel *On the road* in 2009. Like the Morpeth Roll, this took the form of a
long, continuous roll, but of typescript, measuring 36m in length. The
Morpeth Roll presented a different set of challenges, particularly as its exact
length was unknown (it had not been unrolled in its entirety in recent times).
When it was removed from its chest, the roll could clearly be seen wrapped
around the bobbin, lined with a cloth backing on the underside of the paper,
and tied with two pink cords (fig. 59).

---

1 The phrase was used by O'Connell in his speech on 12 August at the Royal Exchange: *Freeman's
Journal*, 13 Aug. 1841.

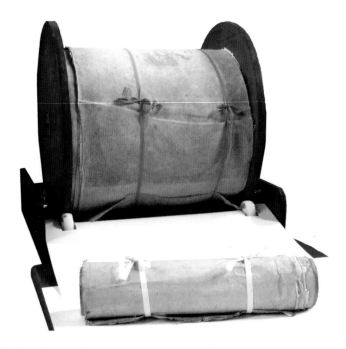

59 The first glimpse of the Morpeth Roll once it had been lifted from its chest.

Once the cords were untied and the roll was unwound, we had our first glimpse of the contents. Among the names of Ireland's political, social, cultural, religious and economic elite appeared those of Thomas Davis and Charles Bianconi, Protestant and Catholic clergy such as Bishop Murphy of Cork, as well as members of the nobility. Many of these names are recognizable to the student of history, but the majority of signatures represent ordinary Irish people who are less well known. There were Ryans of Tipperary, Kehoes of Wexford and Dohertys of Armagh (fig. 60). There were also names in Irish like Sean McCormic written in the Irish hand, and odd names like 'Barney Horse'. In a patriarchal society, one would not expect to find any women signing the testimonial, but a Mary Kenny appears to have done so (fig. 61).[2] It was immediately apparent that the roll was a unique, rich and hitherto unknown record of society in pre-Famine Ireland, but that comprehending it would demand the attention of political, social, local and family historians, as well as conservators, calligraphers and historians of paper,

2 Tim O'Neill, calligrapher, concurs with the view that this is a woman's signature.

60 Signatures including one name in an Irish hand.

61 Signature of Mary Kenny, one of the very few women to have signed the roll.

and also specialists in digitization. The role of the conservation unit in the Russell Library has been to investigate the physical make-up of the object, to prepare it for digital imaging, and to carry out remedial repairs.

The first task was to discover just how many sheets made up the roll and what was its approximate length. This information would allow us to draw up a plan for the artefact's preservation, digitization and display, and allow us to assess its current physical condition. One disturbing hint lay at the bottom of the chest when the bobbin was removed for the first time; this was a scrap of dirty paper with evidence of mould growth and insect damage (fig. 62). It was a fragment from the roll, but it was not clear if this was an isolated instance of damage or if it was symptomatic of something worse. The bobbin was removed to the conservation studio, where the first thought was to unroll the sheets entirely onto another newly made spool. This proved unsuccessful, because the paper did not unwind evenly, and as the sheets wrapped around the new spool they began to veer off centre. In the past, this action had caused their edges to ride up onto the inner sides of the spool and become creased and torn (fig. 63). These practical difficulties led us to wonder when the roll

62 Backlit fragment showing silverfish damage; silverfish thrive in damp conditions.

63 Damage to the edge of the sheets that have become crushed and torn against the side of the bobbin when being wound up.

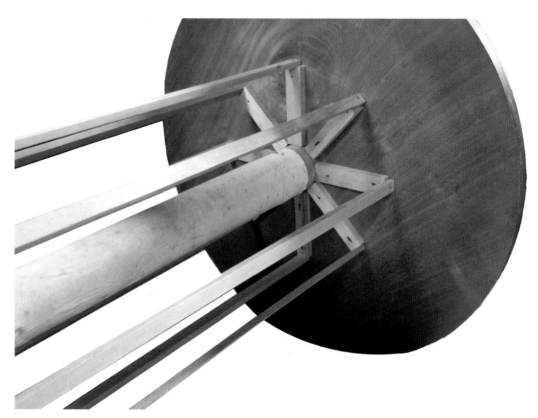

64 The axle at the centre of the bobbin. The inner axle, lined with paper, was modified at a later date by the introduction of the outer arrangement of eight wooden laths.

had last been unwound. It was not clear at this stage if it had ever been completely unrolled since the moment of its presentation in 1841.

As more of the roll was unwound, breaks began to appear: it was evidently not still in one huge, intact length. At various points, sheets had become torn and detached from one another, and in the light of this it was decided to temporarily separate out these segments. In total, there were forty-two breaks or complete tears, and each of these portions was wrapped around a cardboard tube lined with acid-free paper. These mini-rolls had a huge advantage in terms of ease of handling, which had been a major issue up to this point. But the practical solution of creating the mini-rolls caused another serious headache in relation to recording and numbering the sheets in their correct sequence. As it was unwound, each sheet was numbered in pencil in the top right corner. The roll was unwound from the start of the document, beginning with the address to Morpeth, but occasionally sheets would come out in reverse order, with the text upside down to the rest of the document. For these sheets, the number appeared in the bottom left corner. These breaks in the roll, and the fact that some fragmentary sections seemed to have been wound back onto the bobbin in reverse order, were strong evidence for the roll having been unwound and handled subsequent to its creation. A small number of sheets contained signatures or markings on their reverse, and these had to be recorded as part of the true sequence. Elsewhere, smaller pieces of the roll came to light, some were half sheets, others no bigger than thin strips. These were designated as fragments and given a corresponding number.

The paper sheets were reasonably uniform in size, measuring approximately 56cm wide and 65cm long. A standard width was necessary if the sheets were to wind around the bobbin comfortably, but even the small variations in width contributed to the difficulty in spooling the paper in a tidy, uniform manner. Once all the calculations were made, the roll measured a massive 420m and contained 652 sheets, plus the fragments. On reaching the centre of the bobbin, it was a relief not to have found any contamination in the form of mould or infestation. But the central structure of the bobbin itself was also beginning to pose interesting questions and difficulties. The axle in the middle was constructed from thin, evenly spaced wooden laths connected to an inner axle (fig. 64). The result of this curious construction was that the space available for containing the wound sheets of paper on the bobbin was significantly reduced. What was the reason for this?

We began to speculate whether the sheets of paper had once been attached to the inner axle. Alternatively the outer laths might have been designed to bulk out the volume of the roll so that when fully wound up the sheets of paper would be nearly flush with the outer edges of the bobbin, thereby giving it the appearance of being larger and longer, and more impressive. These conjectures were typical of the kinds of enquiry we were voicing at each stage of the investigation. One of the mysteries and delights of the Morpeth Roll is that it provokes so many questions and relatively few answers. We had already established that the order of the roll had been disturbed to the point where it seemed to be positively chaotic. The difficulties here were compounded by the size and volume of the object. It is unusual in conservation to work on a massively oversized book or document; it is nearly always possible to have an overall view of the object in question. This was not the case with the Morpeth Roll, where we would have needed a space the size of an aircraft hangar with a gantry above in order to get a bird's-eye view of it in its entirety.

At 420m, the roll is 100m longer than the tallest structure in Ireland, the Strabane transmitting station in Co. Tyrone. It is 60m longer than the Emely Moor transmission tower in West Yorkshire, the tallest structure in the United Kingdom; and it is almost seven times longer than the height of Liberty Hall in Dublin. Working on an object of this size was unprecedented, and would require special procedures if we were going to piece it together as it was originally assembled, and see if anything was missing.

One of the next tasks was to assess the condition of the roll once it had been removed from the spool. Not surprisingly, dust and dirt had become ingrained over the years. Tears and creases and some paper loss were evident as a result of it being wound and unwound in the past; further evidence that it had been consulted in the interim. There can be no doubt that the most popular part of the roll was the opening address and the sheets immediately following it. These first forty-five sheets had been lined with a cloth backing, and closer inspection revealed finger marks at the head of the first sheet. As the most important part of this family heirloom, it was quite likely to have been shown off at intervals by the family at Castle Howard.[3] What was perhaps more surprising was that much deeper within the roll there was evidence that these sections had been consulted too, even to the extent of candle grease stains being occasionally present. As we had found out in the Russell Library, unrolling the document was comparatively easy; the real problems lay with winding the sheets back onto the bobbin. Previous members of the Howard family must have encountered the same difficulty.

Examination of the paper used on the roll revealed more clues. The early sheets, including the address, are of a heavy type, and they have been well calendered, thereby presenting a very shiny surface. Calendering is the process by which sheets of paper are pressed by rollers to glaze or smooth the surface. Consequently, the inks tend to rest on the surface and do not penetrate the paper. These early sheets had once been backed with a mull cloth (a thin muslin); at a later stage, this had been removed, and a replacement cotton backing had been applied to the first fifteen sheets. Animal glue had been used originally to attach the mull to the back of the paper; it was of a poor quality, contaminated with dirt and had deteriorated with time. As a result, the glue appears to have stiffened the mull, giving it an abrasive feel while at the same time staining the paper with contaminants (fig. 65). Because the winding and unwinding process meant that the surface of each sheet would

---

3 In his acceptance speech, Morpeth referred to the roll as 'the richest heirloom' he could bequeath his family: *Pilot*, 15 Sept. 1841.

65 Removing the cloth backing on the early sheets; because the adhesive had degraded, this came away easily. With each winding of the roll, the inks on the surface would rub against the underside of the cloth causing abrasions.

wrap around the underside of the previous sheets, this rubbing action abraded the inks and produced a fine dust every time the bobbin was turned.

Further into the roll, the paper is of a lighter constitution and appears to have been from batches sent around the country to be signed by people in various localities. Unlike the early lengths, some sheets in this section are so thin that the inks have penetrated through to the reverse side of the paper. There were a number of sheets with watermarks, showing them to have been produced by Lloyds of Monmouthshire in Wales, whose short-lived business had a reputation for producing good quality papers used by the government in its colonial offices worldwide; today, Lloyd papers can be found in Australian government archives, for example (fig. 66).[4] The use of Lloyd's

4 George Lloyd, in partnership with William Williams, operated Whitebrook Upper Mill in Monmouthshire between 1828 and 1839: Alfred Shorter, 'Paper mills in Monmouthshire', *Archaeologia*

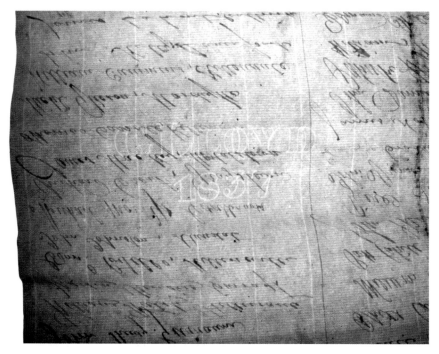

66 G. Lloyd watermark, 1837.

paper prompts the conjecture that there was a shortage of paper in the Dublin area for this project, and that government offices supplied the paper from old stock that had been discontinued.

The presence of repairs to the paper raised the question of whether these were carried out when the roll was first assembled or later (fig. 67). At a time when paper was expensive, and in high demand, it is not surprising to find it being recycled; this was a long-established practice. Recycled paper strips have been used on the Morpeth Roll to join two sheets together, and there are many instances of small strips of extra signatures pasted in (figs 68, 69). The information about how the paper was used was very helpful, but unfortunately it did not get us any closer to establishing how the roll looked when it was first compiled, or how long it was. What does seem clear is that it has at some point suffered damage and loss, but this is hard to quantify without more substantial evidence.

Cambrensis, 102:2 (1953), 83–8. G. Lloyd watermarks are known but are not common. Lloyd was a member of a well-established papermaking family that operated other mills in Monmouthshire and several mills in Gloucestershire at the end of the eighteenth century and the first half of the nineteenth century. This information is courtesy of Mr Peter Bower, expert in paper history and analysis.

67 An old repair, the date of which remains unknown.

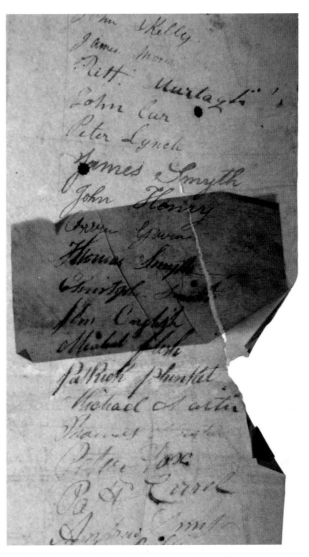

67 An old repair, the date of which remains unknown.

The inks that were used tell us something about how the roll was stored, and how it might have suffered damage and loss. Both ink and paper react to environmental conditions, but since the roll has been stored in a chest, light damage can be ruled out as a cause of the iron gall ink fading. Ink can be chemically unstable, and the quality can also determine how well it survives. Although there are some local instances of water staining, generally the inks on the roll do not exhibit the tell-tale halo effect (leeching, as the ink spreads into the paper) that would indicate damp storage conditions over a long period. If pervasive damp can be discounted as a factor in the deterioration of

68 Reused strips of signatures have been used to join sheets together.

69 Additional strips of paper containing signatures have been pasted onto the verso of the roll under the cloth backing.

sections of the roll, then this raises the possibility that it suffered a single catastrophic event. Such an event would have resulted in some measure of paper loss, as had all along been indicated by the fragment found in the base of the chest. But it was still not possible to ascertain how much paper had been lost.

The opening address to Morpeth is the most ornate part of the entire document, it is inscribed in a fine calligraphic hand and there is evidence that it was originally decorated with colours including gold. It is still possible to

70 The farewell address to Morpeth. Once, it would have been richly coloured, but this decoration has faded over time and through rubbing against the cloth backing.

The Right Honorable
Lord Viscount Morpeth

THE ADDRESS
of the
Nobility, Gentry, Clergy, Merchants, Traders &
PEOPLE of IRELAND

My Lord

We The Reformers of Ireland convened by Public Requisition, for the purpose of considering the most suitable means of manifesting our high respect for your Political Character, and our cordial attachment towards yourself personally, cannot permit Your Lordship (with our recollection of recent events) to terminate that Official connexion with our Country which has happily existed for more than six years, without tendering to Your Lordship formally, the assurance of the profound respect and affection which we entertain towards Your Lordship.

We held in our grateful remembrance the devoted zeal with which, in early life — in those dark days of bondage, when a vast majority of our fellow Countrymen were oppressed for Conscience sake.— Your Lordship ranged yourself with the Friends of Ireland; — And we have marked the earnestness with which Your Lordship has ever since essayed to impart life and spirit to the cold form of Civil and Religious Enfranchisement which you and others had created.

During your Official career in Ireland, it has been your happy destiny to assist in those good measures of policy, whose object has been to raise Ireland to a just equality with other portions of the Empire.— And we venture to affirm that your mind will derive a solace in your retirement from the fact which we now proclaim, that under the Government of which you have been a part, the social state of Ireland has continuously improved, and that a more animated Loyalty and Allegiance to our gracious and beloved Sovereign have been established, than existed towards a Monarch, at any former period in history, since the commencement of British Connexion.

To recapitulate the various Acts of Public Service which Your Lordship has accomplished in Ireland, would far exceed the limits prescribed to an occasion like the present. To enumerate the beneficent designs in which Your Lordship has been engaged, but which have been instead abortive by the hostility of the Enemies of Ireland, would still more transcend the boundary which we have defined for our immediate purpose.— Let Your Lordship be assured, that the People of Ireland treasure in their Hearts, the recollection of every benefit designed for the amelioration of their Country.—

To such of us as have enjoyed the opportunity of personal communication with Your Lordship, it may be permitted, to express our fond recollection of the kindliness of disposition, and the frank and Courteous Demeanour which adorn your private intercourse.— Eminent indeed must be these qualities, to which we, your Friends, admit, when their existence in your person receives, even from your Adversaries, a full acknowledgment.

We cannot retire from Your Lordship's presence, without adverting to the recent event which has removed Your Lordship from the House of Commons, and giving expression to our hope, that no temporary impediment may turn Your Lordship from those walks of honor and Public Utility, in which it has hitherto been your pride to travel.— It may be My Lord, that in this hope, there lurks some element, not entirely free from selfishness — these are not times, My Lord, when Ireland can spare, from her friendly ranks, a Defender so Chivalrous and Brave, as she has proved Your Lordship, the encounter with her Enemies

71 The oily, wagon-wheel mark on the cloth support.

see cuts to the head and tail of the two sheets used for the address, and these slits have a pinhole in the centre. It seems likely, therefore, that the address was pinned to a wall alongside the names of the nobility and that a ribbon was fed through the slits as a decorative feature. The paper does have a watermark, and we know it was produced by Whatman. The colours have long since faded, and the stiffened mull is most likely to have been responsible for this, abrading the colours as the roll was wound and unwound (fig. 70). The glue also caused significant damage to the appearance of the artefact, and there is a further indication of damp of at least a temporary nature. At the centre of sheet five is an oily circular shape that resisted understanding until it could be examined from the other side (fig. 71).

After these preliminary investigations, we paused to summarize the evidence so far. We had a long, linear artefact that defied an overall visual survey because of its size. We had measured its length and numbered its sheets. We knew that there were a number of different types of paper – the better quality paper was to the front and included the address, and this early part was lined with two types of cloth. The lighter papers were to be found

72 Faintly visible on the underside of this section is the pencil signature of John Rowland, upholsterer in Malton, dated 1841.

later in the roll. It seems to have been consulted, especially the opening address along with the signatures on the first few sheets. There had been considerable difficulty in rolling it back onto the spool, which had resulted in tears and creases. Storage appears to have been good, but there might have been a moment of sustained deterioration, and damaged sheets have been cannibalized to repair parts of the roll and infill other parts. Finally, we had an odd oily mark. The next question was how could this evidence help advance our understanding of the object?

One of the tasks we had set ourselves was to prepare the roll for imaging, and we began by removing the cloth lining to the opening sheets. This might have proved a delicate matter but was not so in this case; the glue had deteriorated and was no longer carrying out its basic adhesive function. The cloth backing was easily peeled away from the underside of the paper. This meant that the reverse of these first sheets was now visible, and this shed new light on the roll. It was clear that cannibalized sheets of paper had been used here also. Most excitingly, we discovered the name, address and date of an upholsterer written in pencil – John Rowland of Malton in Yorkshire (fig. 72). By removing the cloth backing, it was also possible to discern a logo on the mysterious oily stain, in a rough wagon-wheel shape, and it was also clear from signs of scraping that someone had tried to remove this at some

73 The Yorkshire testimonial to Morpeth in the long gallery at Castle Howard. It measures about a quarter of the length of the Irish roll.

point. This led us to wonder if Lord Morpeth, immediately upon his arrival back in Yorkshire, had sent the roll to John Rowland in the nearby town of Malton.[5] But if Rowland was responsible for lining the opening sheets with mull, perhaps he also was responsible for the bobbin to wrap the testimonial around, and the chest and the u-shaped brass brackets that allow the bobbin to wind and unwind. If this were the case, then he would have been responsible for the four gouges on the inside of the box to facilitate the bobbin's rotation.

At this point, it was useful to compare the Irish testimonial with the one presented to Morpeth by his constituents in the West Riding. This exists as a very thick roll of paper (slightly wider than the Irish roll at 66cm); it is not housed in anything, and, regardless of how often it has or has not been consulted, when rolled up it presents an uneven, untidy appearance (fig. 73). We therefore have to ask if Morpeth received the Irish address in a similar form, and if subsequently he decided to house it in an oak chest with a bobbin device. If so, how did he come across this mechanical arrangement,

5 Papers at Castle Howard show that John Rowland worked with a George Beverley in Malton during the 1840s. Bills for their upholstery and joinery work do not mention any chest or bobbin: Castle Howard Archives, F5/6, General Bills, 1843.

74 The mahogany chest with brass plaque on the front commemorating the occasion.

and what precedents were there for wrapping a long roll around a giant bobbin? Or did somebody else, such as Rowland, make this decision for him? On the other hand, the inscription does suggest that the chest was part of the actual presentation in Dublin (fig. 74).

> The Address of the Reformers of Ireland
> To Lord Viscount Morpeth
> Presented by His Grace the Duke of Leinster
> At the Royal Exchange in the City of Dublin
> On Tuesday the 14th Septr. 1841

For the time being, we have to entertain both possibilities. The textual evidence would suggest an Irish origin, but the physical evidence may suggest an alternative explanation. The answer to this question, if it can ever be established, will go a long way to illuminating the various stages of the assembly of the roll and its mechanical accoutrements.

The actual preparation for digitization of the roll was relatively straight-forward. Creases were unfolded and flattened, and difficult tears were secured against further damage. Under the agreement between Castle Howard and Ancestry.com, the digitization was to be part of making the signatures available for online consultation by genealogists all over the world. The photography was carried out by UK Archiving from Edinburgh. Capturing all the sheets took less than a week, and this work was made considerably simpler by the earlier creation of the mini-rolls, which allowed for much greater ease of handling, especially when reverse sections of the paper had to be photographed where they contained signatures, stamps or franking marks. The digitized images allowed us some degree of overview for the first time, and it was now possible to place images of broken sections end-to-end and to match them up virtually instead of having to handle unwieldy sections of rolled up paper. This matching exercise allowed us to recreate the sequence of sheets as they might have appeared in Dublin in 1841. Once these sections had been reunited, we were left with unmatched sections, and, from this, we estimated there to be about six sections or lengths of signatures missing, and these would have stretched across an unknown number of sheets of paper.

At this point, we also reached a fresh set of conclusions about the arrangement of the laths in the centre of the spool. Because there is a direct match between the tear on the final blank sheet of the roll and the remnants attached directly to the spool axle, the roll must at one point have been wound directly around this inner axle. The lath arrangement was probably introduced at the same time as new cloth was added. This was a mercerized or pearled cotton, a product first manufactured and patented in 1844 in Lancashire by John Mercer. It was later developed and improved into its modern form by H.A. Lowe in 1889 (fig. 75). The evidence pointed to the fact that towards the end of the nineteenth century the mercerized cotton replaced the original mull on the opening sheets of the roll, and was also used at the end to strengthen the support around the new arrangement of laths. The presence of a matching paper at both ends proved that the roll *had been* unwound in its entirety at some point for the purposes of this remedial work. The reason for this was probably to replace sections of damaged paper that are now lost. The laths allowed the paper to be bulked out, filling the entire bobbin. By measuring the space between the central axle and the later laths,

75 The mercerized or pearled cotton, which was introduced later with the new arrangement of laths.

we estimated that perhaps as much as 50m of paper had been lost.

These conjectures had to be revised in the light of the results of the electronic indexing of the roll by Ancestry.com, which established that today it contains 157,439 signatures. Inevitably, there was a slight feeling of anti-climax on learning this, but, from a conservation point of view, it seemed to confirm our suspicions that a great deal of the roll had been lost. If we take the contemporary press reports of 257,000 signatures at face value (although we should be wary of giving that figure too much credence), this would mean that perhaps 100,000 signatures have been lost, and this might translate into something in excess of 200m of paper. Unless these lost portions ever turn up, however, it remains impossible to be certain just how much of the roll is missing, and therefore how many signatures it contained, and what its exact length was when presented to Morpeth in 1841.[6]

6 The total of 257,000 is reported in the *Freeman's Journal*, 15 Sept. 1841. The calculation for what might be missing is based on the very crude reckoning that if 157,000 signatures are contained on 420m of paper, 100,000 signatures would require more than half that length. But as the signatures on the roll are by no means in a uniform format, with numbers varying on each sheet, it is difficult to be any more precise than this. The fact remains that substantial amounts of the roll no longer exist.

76 Two blue two-penny stamps and two sets of franking marks on the reverse of a sheet that was posted on 10–11 September 1841 from Ballyboro to the secretaries at the Committee Room in the Commercial Buildings, Dublin. Ballyboro, known today as Bailieborough, is in Co. Cavan.

77 The embossed paper crucifix.

In addition to the paper, ink, cloth, chest and bobbin arrangement, the roll contained other features of interest, including franking marks and in one or two instances actual two-penny blue postage stamps. These postage stamps do not have the perforations associated with later stamps. The perforating machine was patented in 1848 by Henry Archer, a Dublin landowner (fig. 76).[7] There is also a small embossed blue green circle of card with a crucifix and the words 'MY HOPE' attached to the side of a sheet. An unsuccessful attempt was made to remove it sometime in the past, but it is still there (fig. 77).

In conclusion, what we have is a fascinating piece of historical, social and political evidence that may challenge how we have traditionally viewed ourselves. The bobbin and the chest arrangement are unique, and reveal how at some point this mechanical arrangement for consulting the roll was deemed a necessary and practical measure if it was to be unwound and rewound easily. There is enough evidence of handling to suggest that the roll was inspected from time to time and the bobbin arrangement must have facilitated this, even though winding the paper back onto the bobbin was not

7 Henry Archer (1799–1863) was the inventor of the first postage stamp perforating machine, which he patented in 1848, to facilitate stamp separation. His patent for his perforating machine was purchased for £4,000 in June 1853, and new machines based on Archer's principles were constructed by David Napier and Son Ltd. These were initially used in October 1853 for revenue stamps and from January 1854 for postage stamps. A Henry Archer does appear in the list of signatures on the roll.

without its difficulties. There is evidence of paper loss, but equally there are clear signs that great effort was made to save as many of the signatories' names as possible, and this was after Morpeth's death. The artefact is enormously long, containing tens of thousands of names, and it presents great conservation and preservation challenges for the future.

Historical research has begun to explain the moment of its commissioning, and the roll is a godsend for genealogists, whose researches are bound to uncover a great deal more information. It has been especially rewarding to carry out this research and conservation work in parallel with the historical investigation of the roll. The opportunity for these disciplines to inform, support or challenge each other's findings has enriched our understanding of it.

The Morpeth Roll remains a very curious *object*. Our physical investigations have begun to uncover much about its assembly and treatment, but there is still a great deal more to be done. In the future, modern technology will no doubt have a big role to play in confirming or otherwise these initial conclusions.

The Morpeth Roll today

CHRISTOPHER RIDGWAY

THE MORPETH ROLL remains a unique document. As far as we are aware, there is no other farewell address to a nineteenth-century politician of this magnitude and strange construction; it is a very special testimonial to a genuinely popular man, whose 'political ameliorations' in the affairs of Ireland prompted enormous gratitude and affection (fig. 78).[1] It is also, as Patrick Cosgrove has argued, a significant political document that reflects a particular moment in early Victorian Ireland, and, as with most public acts, it contains a number of different agendas on the part of those who organized its creation, signed it and presented it to Morpeth. And the roll is, as Paul Hoary has illustrated, a mechanical object with a convoluted and obscure afterlife (fig. 79). In one respect, the roll is far from being unique; there are many other sets of historical records that can open up an understanding of Ireland at particular moments in history. The Morpeth Roll is not exactly a lost source; rather, it is something that had not been fully recognized before its 'rediscovery' in the archives at Castle Howard. Its status as a document of Irish significance is slightly unusual too: the farewell gift to a departing British official. Its precious and fragile condition adds to its mystique, because it is a survivor. Had it remained in Ireland among state or government papers, it might not have survived the archival ravages of the twentieth century; had it continued to lie in obscurity at Castle Howard, it might eventually have crumbled away.

Beyond the good fortune of its survival, however, what is the significance of the Morpeth Roll today? Its rediscovery at Castle Howard coincided with fresh research into the figure of the seventh earl of Carlisle in 2009, but the existence of the roll, while always vaguely known about, had been

1 The phrase comes from the *Freeman's Journal*, 15 Sept. 1841.

complicated by the accounts of Morpeth's second great testimonial from the West Riding.[2] Historians seem to have conflated the two documents, and not until they were actually placed side-by-side did it become apparent that they were the products of two very different, albeit simultaneous, exercises.[3] Simply to establish that there are two documents has been useful, but it is only following the loan of the Irish testimonial to NUIM that new and significant discoveries have been made.

Historians can comprehend the document as an invaluable window onto pre-Famine Ireland, and in one respect it can act as a pre-Famine census substitute. The information buried within it has much to say about political awareness at a national and local level. The very mechanics behind its rapid creation have things to tell us about transport and communications at that moment, even to the point of supplying information on the Irish postal system from the postage stamps and franking marks on many of the sheets.[4] Buried within the mass of names will be material of interest to local and family historians, and this demographical information may throw light on the social organization of parishes and other localities.

The scope of genealogical enquiry is extensive, and the fact that the document can be investigated in such detail is in itself a mark of the digital era. The collaboration between Castle Howard, NUIM and Ancestry.com has enabled the roll to be researched, conserved and digitized.[5] New technologies mean that researchers can overcome the intractable hurdle of how to handle such a large and unwieldy document. Searching the names electronically can be done from anywhere, as can viewing the signatures on screen. The opportunity to view the roll for real also offers a special experience. Being made out of paper and ink, it may not be as handsome an object as the silver gilt and bog oak wine cooler that Morpeth received from his Yorkshire constituents, but it has infinitely more to say. Like all precious documents, it carries a numinous quality, even though digital access is the only really practical way to consult it. In this respect, the comfortable coexistence of the roll in both paper and virtual form challenges the glib assumptions that the latter is set to displace the former once and for all.[6]

2 This resulted in the exhibition at Castle Howard in 2010, *The pride of Yorkshire: George Howard, an eminent Victorian earl*.   3 Diana Olien speaks of the Yorkshire address containing 257,000 signatures when this is the figure cited by the duke of Leinster for the Irish testimonial; moreover, she claims it was on parchment and four hundred feet long: *Morpeth*, p. 240. But it is not clear if Olien ever saw either document first hand in the archives at Castle Howard.   4 Anthony Hughes at NUIM is currently researching the nineteenth-century post office in Ireland.   5 The Morpeth Roll can be seen and searched on the Ancestry website at www.ancestry.com/Morpeth.   6 Ian Sansom has recently stated that 'reports of the death of paper have been greatly exaggerated', *Paper, an elegy* (London, 2012), p. xvi.

78 The Morpeth Roll with just seven of its 420m unrolled in the Russell Library at NUIM.

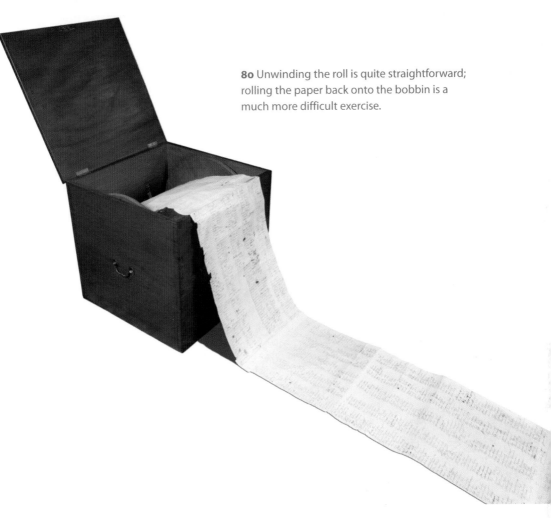

80 Unwinding the roll is quite straightforward; rolling the paper back onto the bobbin is a much more difficult exercise.

All manner of methodological enquiries arise from working with a document of this nature. Not only is there the debate about the value of virtual representation alongside the real object, more fundamentally, there is the question of how one reads the document.[7] Indeed, how was it comprehended in the first place? Perhaps the process of compilation, production and presentation meant more than the finished artefact, let alone how it was ever engaged with subsequently. Notwithstanding the physical evidence uncovered by Paul Hoary, it is hard to think of Morpeth or his descendants regularly rolling out the document in the long gallery at Castle Howard (at 55m, the longest space indoors), and scrutinizing it (fig. 80). Is its meaning therefore defined principally by its status as a public gift on a

7 Sonja Neff asserts that there is no dichotomy between manuscript and mechanical, technical or digital script: *Imprint and trace, handwriting in the age of technology* (London, 2008), pp 19–20.

79 The bobbin resting on spindles inside the chest turn a large document into a mechanical object. The canvas straps are for lifting the bobbin in and out of the chest.

81 Wrapped around the bobbin, the address is transformed into a large cylinder of paper.

grand occasion, and, if so, what significance does the multitude of signatures hold? Perhaps it is the mass that counts, and any sense of individual gratitude and affection is obscured by this multiplicity of names; although for the signatories signing their name would have represented a unique, personal contribution to this mass. The question therefore has to be asked of the Morpeth Roll, was it ever meant to be read? Inspected perhaps, but it is almost inconceivable that it would be studied line-by-line from start to finish. Therefore, its significance lies more in the creation of a handsome, public testimonial and the ritual of presentation. The giving and the receiving established a bond between the Irish people and Morpeth, or so O'Connell and his allies hoped.

This status as a gift is surely one of the reasons it was turned into such a curious contraption. On the bobbin, it becomes a giant cylinder of paper, similar in format to the leviathan petitions gathered by the Chartists (fig. 81). Fresh in many people's minds will have been the spectacle two years earlier in 1839 of the procession through London of the first monster petition. The size of a cartwheel and weighing a third of a ton, this roll contained three miles of paper and boasted more than a million signatures.[8] Morpeth's roll

8 Malcolm Chase, *Chartism: a new history* (Manchester, 2007), p. 73.

was most emphatically not a petition in the sense that the Chartist rolls were. Nevertheless, it had a latent power, reminding all of O'Connell's ability to command widespread support from the enfranchised and the un-enfranchised. In an era when 'signing a petition was an analogue of voting', the assembly of such a multitude of signatures in the form of a tribute to a government official constituted an overtly political act that expressed a particular national sentiment.[9] With regard to Morpeth's testimonial, one might adapt Paul Pickering's observation about Chartist activists: the typical Repealer 'did not sharpen pikes, he collected signatures'.[10] And the impact of these signatures was incremental: one blank sheet was filled with names, as was another, and then these were joined together; and then more were attached. In this way, ten sheets became one hundred sheets, and one hundred names became one thousand and so on. But, at the same time, this multiplicity was contained within a single scroll; the 652 sheets have been joined together to become one document, in effect one gigantic page, and one loud voice (that was echoed in the speeches in the Royal Exchange and Theatre Royal). The magnitude of this singularity would not be so apparent if the 652 sheets were bound together in book form, where the act of turning leaves is to distinguish them one from the other.

Instead of a giant untidy scroll of paper, Morpeth's testimonial was dressed in a box, complete with brass plaque, and crafted into a mechanical object. It could never be mistaken for a petition of the aggrieved: for one, it did not ask for anything. It was therefore a genteel counterpart to the mass Chartist signings. In the grand surroundings of the Royal Exchange, followed by the magnificent banquet in the Theatre Royal, the presentation of the address was a formal, polite and decorous thanksgiving graced by eloquent speeches, where the only jarring note was when part of the staging collapsed (fig. 82). By contrast, the progress of the National Petition through London in May 1839 experienced a somewhat truncated ceremony. The organizers could not decide when exactly to deliver it to parliament, and the roll was ignominiously deposited 'at the foot of the staircase' in the lodgings of MP and industrialist John Fielden. The crowd, anticipating a great march on Westminster, grew very 'dismal' at this halt in affairs and dispersed in a mood of anti-climax. In fact, Fielden and the MP Thomas Attwood presented the roll to parliament a month later, but not before Fielden's landlady had

9 Simon Morgan notes how petitions could reflect civic, local, regional or national identities: 'The reward of public service: nineteenth-century testimonials in context', *Historical Research*, 80:208 (May 2007), 272.   10 Pickering, 'Chartist petitioning in popular politics, 1838–48', 376, 380.

GRAND BANQUET
TO THE RIGHT HON. LORD VISCOUNT
MORPETH,

O N TUESDAY, the 14th SEPTEMBER
Instant, at the

THEATRE ROYAL, HAWKINS'-STREET.

PRESIDENT.

The Most Noble the Marquis of Clanricarde, K.P., &c. &c.

VICE-PRESIDENTS.

The Right Hon. the Earl of Huntingdon.
The Right Hon. the Earl of Fingall.
The Right Hon. the Earl Miltown, K.P.
The Right Hon. the Earl of Charlemont, K.P.
The Right Hon. the Earl of Gosford, G.C.B.
The Right Hon. Lord Lismore.
The Right Hon. Lord Talbot de Malahide.
The Right Hon. Lord Carew.
The Right Hon. Lord Oranmore.
The Right Hon. Lord Lurgan.
The Right Hon. Lord Monteagle.

COMMITTEE.

Count D'Alton, D.L.
Count Fane De Salis, D.L.
The Right Hon. Patrick Bellew, Bart., D.L.
The Right Hon. F. Ponsonby.
The Right Hon. R. L. Sheil, M.P., D.L.
The Right Hon. George Evans
The Right Hon. James Grattan
The Hon. Robert E. Boyle
The Hon. Henry Caulfield, D.L.
The Hon. Robert Gore, M.P., D.L.
The Hon. William Browne, M.P.. D.L.
The Hon. Charles Southwell, D.L.
The Hon. J. C. Westenra, M.P., D.L.
The Hon. R. S. Carew, M.P., D.L.
The Hon. C. Ffrench, D.L.
The Hon. —— Ffrench, D.L.
Sir Valentine Blake, Bart., M.P., D.L.
Sir John Burke, Bart., D L.
Sir Thomas Esmond, Bart., M.P., D.L.
Sir Emanuel Moore, Bart., D.L.
Sir William Somerville, Bart, M.P., D.L.
Sir John Newport, Bart., D.L.
Sir Percy Nugent, Bart., D.L.
Sir Montague L. Chapman, Bart., D.L.
Sir Richard Keane, Bart., D.L.
Sir William Chatterton, Bart., D.L.
Sir Richard Nagle, Bart., D.L.
Sir James Crofton, Bart., D.L.
Sir John Power, Bart, Kilfane, D.L.
Sir John Kennedy, Bart., D.L.

82 Extensive press coverage recorded how the farewell presentation and banquet on
14 September 1841 was an occasion for the great and the good of the day to assemble
and wish him well (the Castle Howard Collection).

complained that it was clogging up one of her outhouses.[11] In Morpeth's case, his valedictory ceremony was smoothly concluded without any awkward hiatus.

If the contemporary meaning of the Morpeth Roll lies with the spectacle of giving and receiving, what of its significance today? It remains a precious family heirloom, and it has also become an archive of great importance, with the potential to reveal much about Ireland in 1841; and it has also become a rich source for genealogical enquiry. By investigating it (as opposed to just admiring it), the roll changes from a symbol to a physical record that can be consulted.[12] It has also acquired a double identity having been digitized. One can inspect the original, redolent with age, wear and tear, but difficult to comprehend; and there is its digital surrogate, quick and easy to access via an electronic index that leads to the signatures on a screen. Indeed, the means exist today with swipe-screen technology to create a life-sized version of the roll on a horizontal screen, where one swipe of the surface would advance the digital sheets of paper. This would offer a very special way of reproducing and comprehending its rolled-up-ness; in contemporary parlance, it would become a smart bobbin.

Historians and genealogists can interact with the roll in ways never imagined by those who commissioned it in 1841, or by Morpeth, its recipient (notwithstanding his use of the term heirloom). How researchers engage with the document today will perforce be very different from how people might have felt about it in 1841, whether they were writing their names or reading the names of others. Questions of how to read the roll, both physically and intellectually, go to the heart of its construction. The scroll format is so different to the codex form that has for centuries been the norm for the book. In the western world, we read across the page from left to right, and turn pages from recto to verso. Not so with the roll, and because it is displayed horizontally, lying on a flat surface, this necessitates an awkward leaning over sideways to read it. Nor is it easy to envisage its entire length: even if one could reach a vantage point for a perfect bird's-eye view the 420m length

11 *Freeman's Journal*, 10 May 1839; *The Times*, 8, 11 May 1839. For the second petition in 1842, the scroll had to be dismembered in order to be carried into the houses of parliament: a suitable metaphor, if ever, for how the government hoped to fragment the phenomenon of mass agitation: Chase, *Chartism*, p. 206.   12 For a discussion on the meaning of such records, including the Australian women's suffrage petition of 1891, which measures 260m, see Eric Ketelaar, 'Cultivating archives: meanings and identities', *Archival Science*, 12 (2012), 19–33. See also Michael Moss, 'Opening Pandora's box: what is an archive in the digital environment?' in L. Craven (ed.), *What are archives? Cultural and theoretical perspectives: a reader* (Aldershot, 2008), pp 71–87.

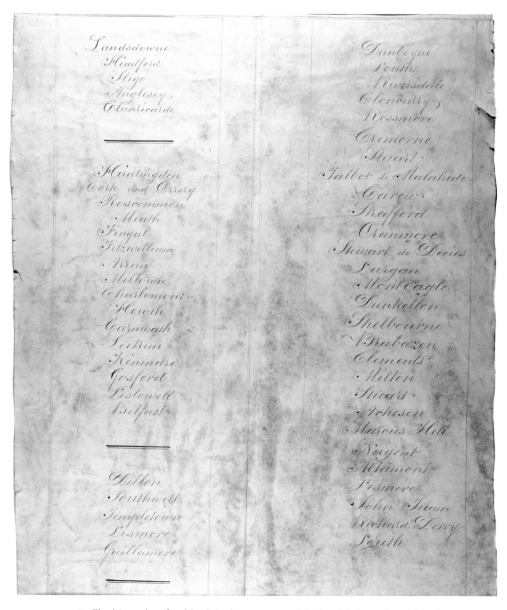

83 The hierarchy of nobles listed in a copperplate hand follows the order of marquesses, earls, viscounts and barons.

would appear no more than a thin, illegible strip. It is a document that paradoxically requires a telescope and a microscope in order to make sense of it. The tendency has been to make comparisons with the length of famous structures: it would extend three times the length of Croke Park in Dublin;

84 A single sheet with miscellaneous signatures in different inks recording names from as far away as Dublin, Kilkenny, Wexford, Tipperary, Galway, Belfast and Armagh.

85 Although compiled in a single hand, this sheet contains names from Kilcock, Maynooth, Waterford, Cork and Limerick.

86 Many signatories have added their occupation on this sheet, including a doctor, a shopkeeper, a merchant, an apothecary, a watchmaker and a shoemaker.

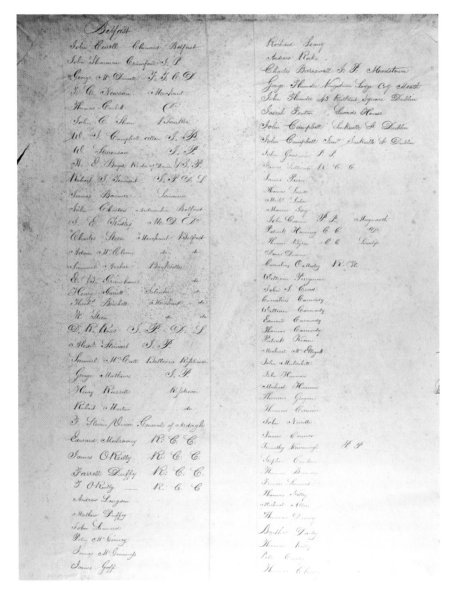

87 A sheet in a single hand. The left column is headed 'Belfast', but the names on the right column are from Dublin and nearby, including Maynooth and Leixlip.

had Morpeth chosen to unroll it on its arrival in Yorkshire he would have found that it was four times the length of his grand home, Castle Howard. But, as Paul Hoary has shown, it makes more sense to understand the roll as a long vertical document; after all it is read in a downward action. This means that analogies with tall structures are more appropriate, perhaps none more arresting than the fact that the roll is just 31m shorter than the Empire State Building.[13]

While access to the document is now straightforward, there remain numerous challenges. One of the biggest difficulties lies with seeing the trees for the wood. Here is a mass of names, but how can we identify who these individuals were? The titled dignitaries are straightforward to identify, as no doubt are clergy, merchants and traders (fig. 83). But what about the 'ordinary' names; who were these people? So many are without identifying tags – a personal signifier or title, an address, a parish or county. But there are plenty of clues within the roll to aid identification, and the expertise and knowledge of local and family history societies will undoubtedly help to excavate many of these names. Clusters of names might reveal specific localities, and these can in turn be checked against other sources, such as Griffith's Valuation, the tithe applotment books or trade directories.

There are sheets filled with miscellaneous signatures in different inks, recording names from different locations. One sheet has people from as far afield as Dorset Street in Dublin, Kilkenny, Wexford, Tipperary, Galway, Belfast and Armagh (fig. 84). Other sheets have a uniform hand, which might suggest one presiding figure, an amanuensis for a locality, but this is not always the case; thus on one sheet the neat hand records people from Kilcock, Maynooth, Kilkenny, Waterford, Dundalk, Cork and Limerick (fig. 85). Some sheets mark the professions of the signatories: a good number are clergy, but there is a strong representation of shopkeepers and manufacturers (fig. 86). In some instances, locations are not always uniform, thus on one sheet, in a single hand, the left column is headed Belfast and followed by the names of justices, clergy, a merchant, a bookseller and other traders. But the right column of the same sheet contains names, in the same hand, from Dublin and nearby, including clergy from Maynooth and Leixlip (fig. 87).

Some localities or parishes are helpfully marked at the top of the sheet: for example, Boyle in Co. Roscommon, and Inchicronan in Co. Clare (figs 88, 89). Parishes in Ulster seem to have been especially well organized, with many of them marked by a little sticker indicating the total number of signatures: for example, 780 names from Upper Creggan, and 431 from Armagh (figs 90, 91). In some instances, the parish priest – clearly responsible for gathering the signatures – has signed himself at the head of the page. Joseph Downes lists

13 Given that it has lost a number of sections, one cannot discount the possibility that the Morpeth Roll was once taller than the Empire State Building.

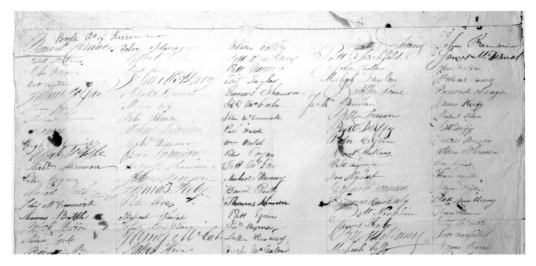

88 A sheet of miscellaneous signatures from the vicinity of Boyle, Co. Roscommon, which is marked in the top left corner.

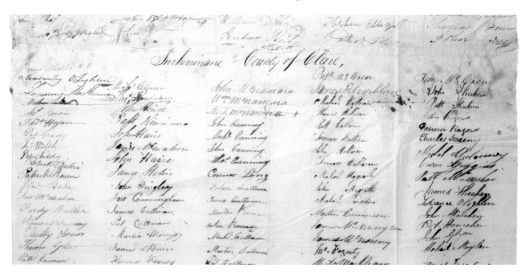

89 A sheet marked 'Inchicronane [sic], County of Clare', with the name of the parish priest at the head of the first column.

several parishes in Tipperary, and Thomas Finney and his curate, William Connolly, sign themselves from Clontibret in Co. Monaghan (figs 92, 93). Even when the priest does not specify his parish, as in the cases of Nicholas Carroll and Joseph Killian, it would not be difficult to trace their whereabouts in 1841, and from this it would be possible to ascertain if the signatories are from that vicinity (figs 94, 95).

90 Ulster parishes frequently added a little sticker to each sheet recording the number of signatures: here, the parish of Upper Creggan gathered 780 names.

91 The parish of Armagh sent in 431 signatures.

Within the sheets, there are other clues and entrées to identifying people and localities. Thus, a sequence of four Murtaghs, each recorded in an identical hand, surely denotes family links at some level, and quite probably geographical proximity (fig. 96). In other instances, there appear eight Sargents and seven Geoghegans each in a uniform hand (figs 97, 98). Some names throw up different complications, however, and there are, inevitably, too many Daniel O'Connells in the roll. The name appears on at least three

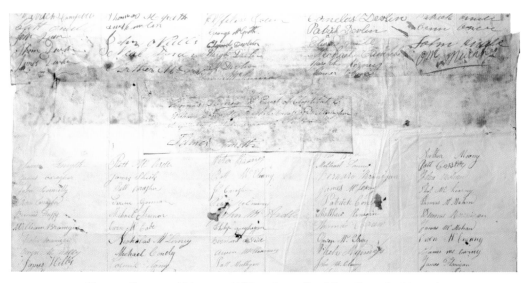

92 Parish priest Joseph Downes gathered names for this sheet from five Tipperary parishes in the barony of Lower Ormond: Knigh, Monsea, Dromineer, Killodiernan and Cloughprior.

93 Thomas Finney and his curate William Connolly of Clontibret, Co. Monaghan, attached a label at the head of this sheet.

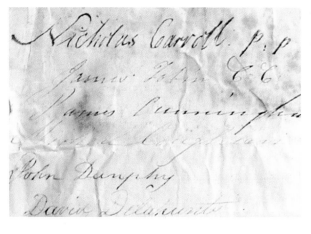

94 This sheet is headed by the name of the parish priest Nicholas Carroll.

95 Joseph Killian OSJ signed his name at the head of this sheet.

different sheets, in one instance among four listed family members (fig. 99). This does not necessarily mean they are fraudulent signatures; as with all popular leaders, the Liberator will have inspired many families to name their sons Daniel.[14] And in case any think that the roll is exclusively a record of the literate, prosperous middle class, there is plenty of evidence of proxy signatures, using the formula of 'X' as a mark. Furthermore, the sheets in a single hand, compiled by priest, schoolmaster or whoever, might easily encompass a wide social spectrum in a locality (fig. 100).

14 There appear to be very few pseudonyms or names that poke fun at authority. Edward Royle points out that in the Chartist petitions many obviously false names were likely to be the result of people wishing to hide their real identity because they feared persecution: *Chartism* (London, 1996), p. 45.

Joseph Graham
John Healy
Patt Hickey
Kieran McDonnell
Patt Rochford
Pat. Jatton
James Bond
Richard Dowling
Denis Murphy
John Kelly
John Murtagh
Mick Murtagh
James Murtagh
John Murtagh
Michael
William Phelan
Phill Dullan
James Costello
William Grace
Owen Fitzpatrick
Mick Shee
Michael Shanahan
Patrick Sullivan

96 Among the miscellaneous signatures on this sheet are four Murtaghs, all signed in the same hand.

97 Signed in a uniform hand are the names of the Sargent family: William (senior), James, Thomas, William (junior), Charles, Daniel O'Connell, George, Frederick George.

Edward Walsh   Patrick Culledon
Francis Cosgrave   Thos Smith
Nichs J. Carttonn   Thomas Burke
Michl Feelin   John Winn
Margaret ?   Patk Spring
                                      Michael Lynch
James Goldrick   James Costello
James Dolan   Maurice Meehan
Joseph McGrane   Peter Farrell
Patt McGrane   Pat Moran
John Mollan   Jno Ferguson
Daniel Farrell   Thos Ryan
James Farrell   Arthr Burke
Patt Higgins
William M. Grainger   John Lurry
John M. Grainger   James Geoghegan
Henry M. Grainger   Francis Geoghegan
Thos M. Grainger   Michael Geoghegan
Jno M. Grainger   John Geoghegan
John Raymond   William Geoghegan
Saml Burel   Charles Geoghegan
James Hennessey   Henry Geoghegan
Stephen Martin   Frank Day
Mathew Brennan   Mathias Mooney
Arthr Johnston   Patt Burke Clontarf
Thos Fogarty   Patt Mulvey

98 Seven members of the Geoghegan family signed this sheet in a single hand:
James, Francis, Michael, John, William, Charles and Henry.

99 O'Connell appears many times on the roll. Here are
Timothy, Cornelius and Daniel.

100 The formula of 'X' against a name appears repeatedly for those who could not write, here identifying Jim Kelly, Andrew Rawden and Patrick McGough; just next to them, William O'Flanaghan has written his name in Gaelic script.

The historical investigation of the roll at this personal and parochial level will uncover much, about both individuals and localities. The 160,000 or so signatures constitute perhaps 2 per cent of the population of 8.2 million people in 1841; however, given that many of these names came from the middle classes, the total represents a higher proportion of educated, prosperous and politically articulate Catholics (as well as Protestants), who would have looked to Dublin Castle to protect their interests. Just before the calamities of the 1840s, this record of signatures acquires a very special status, and one might decide to ask of these names 'What sort of a famine did they have?' If we try to comprehend them across the decade, and not just in terms of this single moment in the summer of 1841, we might justifiably consider the roll a critical Famine document. Questioning where these individuals were at the end of the traumatic 1840s becomes a way of trying to uncover their life stories. What happened to them between 1841 and, say, 1851? Were they alive or dead, prospering or failing, in Ireland or overseas?

By 1841, 28 per cent of the Irish population was literate.[15] Therefore, the act of signing this document, indeed of comprehending it as a special written record in the first place, said something about who you were. The power of the roll lies not just in its age, its size and its unique construction, it also lies with what sits at its heart: the personal signature. Genealogical investigation is about tracing connections, whether these work backwards from the present to distant ancestors, or start from previous times and work forwards through the names of subsequent generations. The activity is about making links, and the roll has the potential to unlock a host of personal histories. For most people, the bridge with one's family past lies with bequeathed images (paintings, miniatures or photographs); precious heirlooms with important associations; or with the written past in the form of letters, diaries, keepsakes and family signatures. Faced with the Morpeth Roll, quite simply, anyone is entitled to ask, 'Is my ancestor on this list?'. Or, to adapt a popular genealogical phrase, one might reflect of that moment in 1841, 'Who did these people think they were?' O'Connell foresaw the testimonial as something that Morpeth could hand down to his descendants; Morpeth concurred and called the roll the 'richest heirloom' his family could have. But the presence of so many signatures means that the roll becomes something of a national heirloom too.

The signature is one of the most basic vestiges of the past, confirming a name and perhaps a point in a lineage. According to Philip Hensher, 'handwriting is what registers our individuality, and the mark which our culture has made on us'.[16] We are our name before anything else (child, adult, spouse; nice person, unpleasant person; famous person, unknown person). And our name is still embedded in our signature. One's handwritten name is proof of one's identity before all else. It is the key to some of the most important documents and actions in people's lives: owning a passport or a driving licence; opening a bank account; possessing the deeds of a house; getting married; making a will. The personal signature is still enormously authoritative and is a requirement in law for many transactions. Yet, in many

15 William J. Smyth, '"Variations in vulnerability": understanding where and why people died' in John Crowley et al. (eds), *Atlas of the great Irish Famine, 1845–52* (Cork, 2012), pp 190–5.   16 Philip Hensher, *The missing ink: the lost art of handwriting (and why it still matters)* (London, 2012), p. 15. This is an entertaining and trenchant account of the fate of handwriting today.

areas of life, the personal signature is fast disappearing. Credit card transactions now require a number and not a signature; before long, written cheques will have disappeared. The advent of email has rendered the written letter and signature unnecessary if not almost obsolete. Will there come a time when identity is no longer confirmed by signature, and, if so, what is the sign that will denote who somebody is? If that moment arrives, will it ever be possible to make such a record as the Morpeth Roll again?

Looking up names and signatures online, as millions of genealogical researchers do, remains the starting point for trying to ascertain who one is and where one comes from. Viewing handwritten documents in exhibitions or libraries or onscreen also testifies to how human script still possesses a power and a fascination, especially if it provides a bridge to one's own past. The names on the roll are flickering Irish presences, each one denotes somebody and establishes that they were there (even though the precise 'there' is not always easy to establish) at a given moment – the summer of 1841. In many cases, these names are traceable, and will confirm a connection with names and families today; whether that person is a recognizable figure in the ancestral chain or a hitherto missing one. It is also possible that in time many of these people will become even more visible, with images added to their names. One day, the roll might conceivably become an illustrated document.[17]

The tour of the roll throughout Ireland starting in 2013 means that these signatures can be seen in public for the first time in 170 years; at the same time, their availability on the Ancestry.com website means that they are accessible to many more people. The tour also coincides with *The Gathering*, which in 2013 is set to celebrate Ireland's past internationally. At the heart of this initiative, which in one sense constitutes a vast genealogical home-coming, lie questions about Irish identity: what does it mean to be Irish today, yesterday or tomorrow? The Morpeth Roll can act as one among many lenses through which to contemplate these questions, and, by asking if the names it contains chose to stay or depart in the 1840s, or left in subsequent decades, or indeed returned at some later point, it acquires a significance that stretches long after 1841 and far beyond the shores of a single island on the western edge of Europe. It has the potential to reach out to millions of people worldwide who claim Irish descent.

17 Ciaran Reilly at NUIM is investigating the emigration papers for the tenants of Strokestown Park, Co. Roscommon, and by contacting descendants today, many of them still overseas, he has begun to match names with images supplied to him.

It is significant that O'Connell spoke of the signatures attesting not the nation but 'the united sentiments of the people of Ireland'. Another year was to pass before Thomas Davis founded the *Nation* newspaper, a moment that signalled a particular milestone in the evolution of national identity, albeit on the eve of a national disintegration by way of famine and emigration. The Morpeth Roll needs to be understood in the context of 1841; and for that period to be satisfactorily comprehended it is necessary to have a knowledge of the previous decade of Whig government in which Morpeth played such a key role. The roll also needs to be understood within wider time frames: firstly across the terrible 1840s, from which one can ask very specific questions about these individuals in the immediate aftermath of the Famine; and then subsequent periods of nineteenth-century history. And at the onset of the twenty-first century, the Morpeth Roll, filled with its multitude of names, can also prompt fresh reflections on a personal and a national past. It presents an opportunity to re-imagine Ireland through the simplest and most fundamental of signifiers – the signature.